Jim **Burke**

5O **essential** *lessons*

Tools *&* **Techniques** *for*
teaching **English Language Arts**

Grades 9–12

Heinemann • Portsmouth, NH

*first*hand
An imprint of Heinemann
A division of Reed Elsevier Inc.
361 Hanover Street
Portsmouth, NH 03801–3912
www.firsthand.heinemann.com

Offices and agents throughout the world

Library of Congress Cataloging-in-Publications Data
CIP data is on file with the Library of Congress

ISBN 0-325-01108-7 (Lesson book)
      0-325-01109-5 (Tools and Texts)
      0-325-00857-4 (set)

Printed in the United States of America on acid-free paper

10 09 08 07 06   ML   1 2 3 4 5 6

TABLE OF CONTENTS

A C K N O W L E D G M E N T S

THIS PROJECT IS THE RESULT of many talented, committed professionals. *50 Essential Lessons* has challenged me to learn new ways of working and aspects of writing, for it is difficult to fit into each lesson all that we wanted to share with you. Throughout this process, I was blessed with a remarkable team of professionals, all of whom contributed important elements to the product in your hands and each of whom I must thank for the "essential lesson" I learned from this project: that such complex work is impossible alone. Thus I express my deep gratitude for the following people:

Leigh Peake, who heads Heinemann's editorial division, pushed me harder than ever, challenging my ideas and filling the whiteboards of the planning room with her wonderful multicolumned, multicolored diagrams that helped me see new possibilities.

Tina Miller, head of *first*hand, guided our team through the march of the past year, listening and responding with great insight and enthusiasm to my emerging ideas, even as she pushed me to clarify my thinking.

Michael Cirone, who managed the whole production, kept it all flowing under often impossible time constraints. I am grateful to Michael for his patience and commitment to the quality of the product.

Charles McQuillen advised me on key aspects of the Teacher's Guide and other elements of design; he also provided helpful advice throughout the process on many other aspects of the project and the *first*hand concept itself.

Ed Stevens did a great job on the page makeup and other aspects of design.

David Stirling served as my mentor for the photography, giving me advice about not only which camera to buy and how to use it but also how to store, organize, and shoot the images.

Cynthia Nye did an incredible job on so many aspects of the project, all of which made a significant contribution to the book. It was Cynthia who combed through all my other books to find the perfect quotations that appear on each lesson, adding not just a nice touch but real substance. I am indebted to Cynthia also for her attention to detail in every lesson: these efforts improved the book and challenged me to rethink aspects of the book at key junctures. She also oversaw the final preparation of the manuscript. Each of these tasks was a job in itself.

Karyn Morrison handled all the permissions work, and for that I am truly grateful.

I am also appreciative of the meticulous work done by Debbie Leighton and her staff at Maine Proofreading Services.

Lisa Fowler created the cover and page design for *50 Essential Lessons* and orchestrated the page makeup. I cannot thank Lisa enough for her commitment to this project, for it was her design, her insight into what the pages could look like and how they could function, that transformed these lessons into something special—and useful. She taught me what design can do, how it can contribute to content if done right. Working with and learning from Lisa was one of the great blessings of this project.

Two people remain, neither of whom I can ever thank enough: my editors Lois Bridges and Lisa Luedeke. Lois has been my editor since my first book; she worked with me on the first half of this project, guiding, challenging, clarifying, and supporting as she always has. This book marks a culmination of sorts, as I included in it all that I have learned from the other books I worked on with Lois. It seems fitting then that she should leave to take a new position halfway through, having safely helped me launch this project: having helped me figure out what I was trying to accomplish and helping me to begin doing that. Then my good fortune was to get the chance to work with Lisa Luedeke as my new editor. Lisa came into the middle of the project and immediately set to work so she could help me on the second half. This book marks the beginning of a new editorial relationship, and I am most grateful for all that Lisa has done on this project.

In the end, final acknowledgments—the ultimate gratitude—are always reserved for those who make every book I write possible: my family and my students. Every book I write depends on the support and encouragement of my wife, Susan, and our three wonderful children, Evan, Whitman, and Nora. As for my students: you see them on every page of this book, all from the same year, thus making these Essential Lessons something of a family album for me, an academic yearbook which tries to capture all that we learned from each other. I hope you learn as much from us as I learned from them.

Jim Burke

LESSON OVERVIEW

50 Essential Lessons: Getting Started

How does this lesson structure reflect my teaching sensibility and approach both to the students and to the topics to be taught?

The Essential Lessons are the result of the ongoing study of my own and others' teaching, which is always guided by the question, *What worked—and why?* I am driven by a commitment to create a meaningful learning experience that provides an instructional context in which I can teach the skills and knowledge students are expected to have when they leave high school. While it may seem simple, dividing my lesson design process into three stages–before, during, and after–was transformative. It gave me a way to be more intentional, to achieve greater instructional consistency and cohesion. Thus the structure outlined in these lessons is the result of a careful study of not only what I do but *when* I do it. As I examined my teaching process, I realized there was an order to it, not one that was prescriptive or limiting but rather logical and helpful. Writing these lessons made me realize the stages in my own process; now that I am aware of them, I feel much more effective and confident in my teaching because I feel as though I have achieved a stable model that helps me determine how to teach what my students must learn.

Why is it important to show my students at work in the classroom?

The students you see on these pages are my students from the year during which I taught all these lessons. The younger ones are freshmen in my ACCESS (Academic Success) program for struggling readers; the older ones are seniors who are in my AP English class. It's worth noting that my district allows anyone to enroll in advanced and AP classes, so the thirty-five seniors in each of my AP classes make for a much more intellectually diverse class than teachers used to find in such classes. Whether in AP or honors, teachers used to be able to focus more on content, confident that the kids came in with the skills needed to succeed; such is no longer the case for many of us around the country. The lessons here, which can be adapted to work with students at all levels, show me teaching both ACCESS students and AP students how to do what school assumes they come in knowing how to do but so often do not. The photographs of my students and me are authentic: nothing staged, just a teacher and his kids doing the daily work of learning. I keep a camera in my pocket to capture images of kids doing the assignment well (i.e., providing an example of what it looks like to do a certain task). Sometimes I use these images in books or workshops; I also use them to create a digital yearbook, which I put together and show at the end of the year as part of a big slide show.

Do I have any special recommendations for getting started?

In my ACCESS classes, we begin with some of the Managing Oneself lessons, as the most urgent lessons they need are those that will help them to be organized and to succeed in their academic classes. So I would say that the order in which you use the lessons depends on who you

The preview section of each lesson provides the professional understandings that shaped the lesson. This will help situate the lesson in your curriculum, and it will provide you with the information needed to jump in and get started.

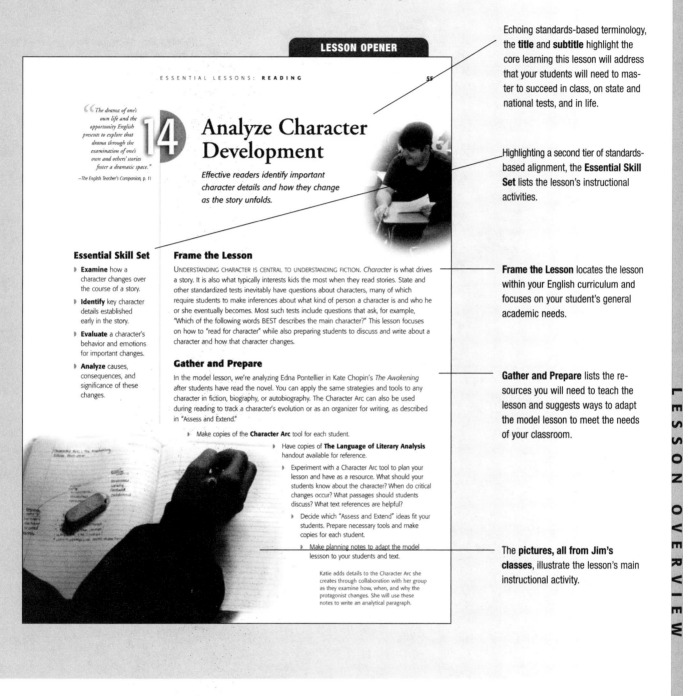

LESSON OPENER

ESSENTIAL LESSONS: **READING**   55

"*The drama of one's own life and the opportunity English presents to explore that drama through the examination of one's own and others' stories foster a dramatic space.*"

—*The English Teacher's Companion,* p. 11

14 Analyze Character Development

Effective readers identify important character details and how they change as the story unfolds.

Essential Skill Set

▶ **Examine** how a character changes over the course of a story.

▶ **Identify** key character details established early in the story.

▶ **Evaluate** a character's behavior and emotions for important changes.

▶ **Analyze** causes, consequences, and significance of these changes.

Frame the Lesson

UNDERSTANDING CHARACTER IS CENTRAL TO UNDERSTANDING FICTION. *Character* is what drives a story. It is also what typically interests kids the most when they read stories. State and other standardized tests inevitably have questions about characters, many of which require students to make inferences about what kind of person a character is and who he or she eventually becomes. Most such tests include questions that ask, for example, "Which of the following words BEST describes the main character?" This lesson focuses on how to "read for character" while also preparing students to discuss and write about a character and how that character changes.

Gather and Prepare

In the model lesson, we're analyzing Edna Pontellier in Kate Chopin's *The Awakening* after students have read the novel. You can apply the same strategies and tools to any character in fiction, biography, or autobiography. The Character Arc can also be used during reading to track a character's evolution or as an organizer for writing, as described in "Assess and Extend."

▶ Make copies of the **Character Arc** tool for each student.

▶ Have copies of **The Language of Literary Analysis** handout available for reference.

▶ Experiment with a Character Arc tool to plan your lesson and have as a resource. What should your students know about the character? When do critical changes occur? What passages should students discuss? What text references are helpful?

▶ Decide which "Assess and Extend" ideas fit your students. Prepare necessary tools and make copies for each student.

▶ Make planning notes to adapt the model lesson to your students and text.

Katie adds details to the Character Arc she creates through collaboration with her group as they examine how, when, and why the protagonist changes. She will use these notes to write an analytical paragraph.

Echoing standards-based terminology, the **title** and **subtitle** highlight the core learning this lesson will address that your students will need to master to succeed in class, on state and national tests, and in life.

Highlighting a second tier of standards-based alignment, the **Essential Skill Set** lists the lesson's instructional activities.

Frame the Lesson locates the lesson within your English curriculum and focuses on your student's general academic needs.

Gather and Prepare lists the resources you will need to teach the lesson and suggests ways to adapt the model lesson to meet the needs of your classroom.

The **pictures, all from Jim's classes,** illustrate the lesson's main instructional activity.

L E S S O N   O V E R V I E W

teach and where they are when they come into your class. I don't say, for example, I need to teach kids how to write today or how to do a character analysis this week. Instead, I might ask what ideas we need to explore and which texts can help us do that. Then in the context of that unit, I would ask myself what skills or knowledge they need to complete the work on that unit. If we are reading a novel such as Chopin's *The Awakening,* for example, which is

very character-driven, I will then turn to the lesson on how to analyze a character. Often we have done this before, but now I am turning to the lesson because I want to challenge them to get to the next level or because I have students who are struggling and I need some way to guide them through the forest of their confusion. On such occasions, I turn to the lessons, as one does to a toolbox, to find a solution to that current instructional problem.

The Teach section chronicles the model lesson's teaching moves and language. The specificity of the narrative allows for a sort of demonstration teaching. You can "listen in" and observe Jim's teaching.

Designed and piloted in Jim's own classroom, each lesson can be completed within a **50-minute period.**

The **instructional narrative** models the types of classroom discussions this lesson will generate and chronicles the interactions that emphasize what Jim says, does, or thinks as the lesson unfolds.

Teaching moves subdivide and offer additional guidance and support for the lesson.

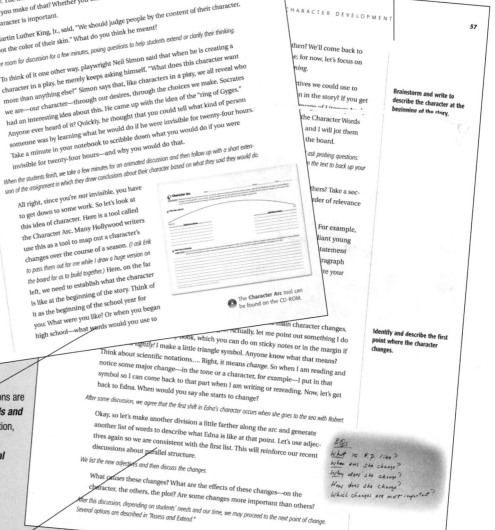

Developed in a low-tech classroom, the lessons require only the most **basic teaching tools**: paper, whiteboard, and overheads. Samples of the work the class generates are shown at point of use.

ESSENTIAL LESSONS: READING

56

Teach

Get kids thinking about character.

CHARACTER IS ONE OF THE MOST FASCINATING ASPECTS OF STORIES, but it's also an interesting idea. The word *character* itself comes from the Greek and means "to inscribe," or "the sharp end of a stick." It makes sense if you think about it: a letter in the alphabet is a "character" and has to be written with a pencil, that is, "a sharp stick." But it also raises an interesting question: If character is our personality, the essence of who we are, then is that "inscribed" into us? Is it written (with "the sharp end of a stick") into our DNA, our code? Or do *we* determine who we are? Do we write the code through our choices, which shape our personality? Or is it both? Character seems to be on people's minds a lot these days. A new book recently came out titled *Character Is Destiny.* The most looked-up word at *Merriam-Webster.com* this year was *integrity*—what do you make of that? Whether you think it comes from our DNA, our choices, or both, character is important.

Martin Luther King, Jr., said, "We should judge people by the content of their character, not the color of their skin." What do you think he meant?

I make room for discussion for a few minutes, posing questions to help students extend or clarify their thinking.

Write to make personal connections.

To think of it one other way, playwright Neil Simon said that when he is creating a character in a play, he merely keeps asking himself, "What does this character want more than anything else?" Simon says that, like characters in a play, we all reveal who we are—our character—through our desires, through the choices we make. Socrates had an interesting idea about this. He came up with the idea of the "ring of Gyges." Anyone ever heard of it? Quickly, he thought that you could tell what kind of person someone was by learning what he would do if he were invisible for twenty-four hours. Take a minute in your notebook to scribble down what you would do if you were invisible for twenty-four hours—and why you would do that.

When the students finish, we take a few minutes for an animated discussion and then follow up with a short extension of the assignment in which they draw conclusions about their character based on what they said they would do.

Use the Character Arc tool to analyze a fictional character.

All right, since you're *not* invisible, you have to get down to some work. So let's look at this idea of character. Here is a tool called the Character Arc. Many Hollywood writers use this as a tool to map out a character's changes over the course of a season. *(I ask Erik to pass them out for me while I draw a huge version on the board for us to build together.)* Here, on the far left, we need to establish what the character is like at the beginning of the story. Think of it as the beginning of the school year for you: What were you like? Or when you began high school—what words would you use to

The **Character Arc** tool can be found on the CD-ROM.

CHARACTER DEVELOPMENT

57

then? We'll come back to ...e; for now, let's focus on ...ning.

...tives we could use to ...n in the story? If you get ...ange of *Literary Ang...* ...the Character Words ...and I will jot them ...the board.

...ask probing questions: ...n the text to back up your

...thers? Take a sec- ...order of relevance

...For example, ...liant young ...tatement ...ragraph ...te your

Brainstorm and write to describe the character at the beginning of the story.

...e main character changes. Actually, let me point out something I do ...book, which you can do on sticky notes or in the margin if *...rightly!* I make a little triangle symbol. Anyone know what that means? Think about scientific notations.... Right, it means *change.* So when I am reading and notice some major change—in the tone or a character, for example—I put in that symbol so I can come back to that part when I am writing or rereading. Now, let's get back to Edna. When would you say she starts to change?

After some discussion, we agree that the first shift in Edna's character occurs when she goes to the sea with Robert.

Okay, so let's make another division a little farther along the arc and generate another list of words to describe what Edna is like at that point. Let's use adjectives again so we are consistent with the first list. This will reinforce our recent discussions about parallel structure.

We list the new adjectives and then discuss the changes.

What *causes* these changes? What are the effects of these changes—on the character, the others, the plot? Are some changes more important than others?

After this discussion, depending on students' needs and our time, we may proceed to the next point of change.
Several options are described in "Assess and Extend."

Identify and describe the first point where the character changes.

B.Q.s
What is E.P. like?
When does she change?
Why does she change?
How does she change?
Which changes are most important?

All of the teaching tools used in the lessons are provided in a reproducible format in *Tools and Texts for 50 Essential Lessons.* In addition, these tools are provided in a convenient PDF format on the *Tools for 50 Essential Lessons CD-ROM.*

To make the teaching as concrete and tangible as possible, **model lessons** draw on texts common to the high school English classroom. The details in these lessons are intended to provide thoughtful, reflective teaching in ways that will help you adapt the strategies and methodologies to your own texts, students, and teaching style.

Each four-page lesson concludes with strategies for how to use assessment to monitor student learning and guide future teaching.

Responses to lessons are as diverse as the students in your class. These strategies suggest ways to provide students with **extra support** or **extra challenge**.

Extension strategies link the lesson to the literacy curriculum and prepare students for subsequent tests.

In addition to tools required by the lesson, *Tools and Texts for 50 Essential Lessons* also contains a rich array of tools that will help you reinforce and extend the lesson. The *Tools for 50 Essential Lessons* CD-ROM provides each tool in an electronic format that is easy to read and print out.

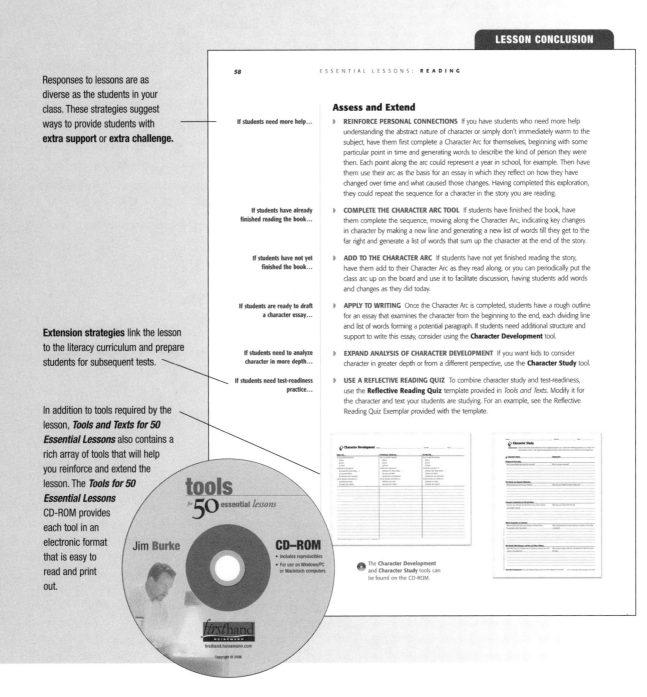

LESSON CONCLUSION

58   ESSENTIAL LESSONS: **READING**

Assess and Extend

If students need more help…

▶ **REINFORCE PERSONAL CONNECTIONS** If you have students who need more help understanding the abstract nature of character or simply don't immediately warm to the subject, have them first complete a Character Arc for themselves, beginning with some particular point in time and generating words to describe the kind of person they were then. Each point along the arc could represent a year in school, for example. Then have them use their arc as the basis for an essay in which they reflect on how they have changed over time and what caused those changes. Having completed this exploration, they could repeat the sequence for a character in the story you are reading.

If students have already finished reading the book…

▶ **COMPLETE THE CHARACTER ARC TOOL** If students have finished the book, have them complete the sequence, moving along the Character Arc, indicating key changes in character by making a new line and generating a new list of words till they get to the far right and generate a list of words that sum up the character at the end of the story.

If students have not yet finished the book…

▶ **ADD TO THE CHARACTER ARC** If students have not yet finished reading the story, have them add to their Character Arc as they read along, or you can periodically put the class arc up on the board and use it to facilitate discussion, having students add words and changes as they did today.

If students are ready to draft a character essay…

▶ **APPLY TO WRITING** Once the Character Arc is completed, students have a rough outline for an essay that examines the character from the beginning to the end, each dividing line and list of words forming a potential paragraph. If students need additional structure and support to write this essay, consider using the **Character Development** tool.

If students need to analyze character in more depth…

▶ **EXPAND ANALYSIS OF CHARACTER DEVELOPMENT** If you want kids to consider character in greater depth or from a different perspective, use the **Character Study** tool.

If students need test-readiness practice…

▶ **USE A REFLECTIVE READING QUIZ** To combine character study and test-readiness, use the **Reflective Reading Quiz** template provided in *Tools and Texts*. Modify it for the character and text your students are studying. For an example, see the Reflective Reading Quiz Exemplar provided with the template.

The **Character Development** and **Character Study** tools can be found on the CD-ROM.

tools *for* 50 essential *lessons*

Jim Burke   **CD–ROM**
• Includes reproducibles
• For use on Windows/PC or Macintosh computers

*first*hand
HEINEMANN
firsthand.heinemann.com
Copyright © 2006

LESSON OVERVIEW

What role does assessment play in these Essential Lessons?

Assessment begins by asking what students need to learn in order to do what I and the larger society expect of them. As these kids, representing such a wide range of levels, enter my class, I must also assess their current level of performance and which instructional method would be most effective for them and their situation. Once I have assessed their needs, I turn to the lessons and tools, choosing those most appropriate to the instructional situation, using the lesson to teach them the necessary skills so they can complete the larger academic demands of the class. As they work, I must also assess their emerging understanding of the material or their proficiency at the skill and make necessary adjustments. In the Assess and Extend section of each lesson, I determine what they need next based on the information their performance provides. In some cases, they require reteaching to help them better understand or reapply the skills I was teaching; others pick it up or start at a higher level, which allows me to extend the lesson to higher levels of sophistication, during which I must assess how they are progressing and determine when we have extended the lesson as far as possible while keeping it educationally valuable.

What should teachers take away from a lesson? Once the lesson is over, we often find ourselves wondering, "What next?" The best answer is that it depends on students' needs, available time, instructional goals, or the content of the class and what would be most effective. If, for example, you are teaching them to "write to define" and find their writing lacking focus, you might interrupt that lesson to use a separate lesson on teaching effective paragraphs and then, having addressed that, resume the larger writing assignment. On another occasion, you might find yourself upon finishing one lesson, wondering what to do next; the table of contents listing the lessons can serve as a useful guide to other aspects of the curriculum you can address through the lessons. The truth is that our work is nonlinear, forcing us to find solutions to problems as they emerge. The lessons thus help me—and, I hope, you—solve several problems that cluster together: What am I supposed to teach? How do I actually teach that? What do I do when, while teaching one thing, I realize students need to learn other skills first to complete the larger task?

Tools can be found on the accompanying CD–ROM.

Texts marked with an asterisk (*) can be found in *Tools & Texts*. Other listed text titles are those used in Jim's model lessons and can typically be found in English classroom resource collections.

ESSENTIAL LESSON MATRIX

Essential Performance	Text	Tool
TEACHER'S GUIDE	Figures 1.1, 1.2, 1.3, 1.4	Lesson Planning Template
READING		
1. **Make connections**	Students' sustained silent reading (SSR) books	Making the Connection
2. **Use a reading process**	* "The Second Coming" (Yeats)	Episodic Notes Reading Process Self-Evaluation
3. **Develop a purpose question**	* "Robo-Legs"	Article Notes
4. **Identify main ideas and supporting details**	* "Burp, Rumble, Toot!"	Main Idea Organizer
5. **Draw conclusions from what you read**	* "Messages from the Heart"	Main Idea Organizer Drawing Conclusions Organizer
6. **Make inferences about deeper meanings**	* "Jesuit Greg Boyle: Gang Priest"	Inference Quiz Making Inferences Organizer
7. **Analyze the author's argument**	* "Could it be that video games are good for kids?"	Argument Organizer Understanding Arg.: An Overview
8. **Examine the author's purpose**	* "The Time 100: Bruce Lee"	Academic Writing Rhetorical Notes
9. **Visualize what you read**	* "Sonnet 116" (Shakespeare) * "Sonnet 18" (Shakespeare)	Visualizing Strategies
10. **Examine multiple perspectives**	*Ophelia* painting, (Millais, Hughes, Waterhouse) *Hamlet*, Act 4, Scene 7 (Shakespeare)	Three-Column Organizer Conversational Roundtable Target Tool
11. **Examine the structure of a text**	*Heart of Darkness* (Conrad)	Plot Notes Time Line Notes Narrative Design Organizational Patterns
12. **Ask questions about what you read**	*Heart of Darkness* (Conrad)	Text Tool Character Study Active Reading: Questions Literature Circle Notes: Overview

cont. on next page

ESSENTIAL LESSON MATRIX

Essential Performance	Text	Tool
12. Ask questions about what you read (continued)	*Heart of Darkness* (Conrad)	Dense Question Strategy Style Analysis Notes Summary of Basic Questions Structured Response Notes Bookmark: Reading A & B Four Core Questions
13. Use the language of literary analysis	*The Awakening* (Chopin)	Language of Literary Analysis Reflective Reading Quiz Reflective Reading Quiz (Exemplar)
14. Analyze character development	*The Awakening* (Chopin)	Language of Literary Analysis Character Arc Character Development Character Study Reflective Reading Quiz Reflective Reading Quiz (Exemplar)
15. Analyze the author's style	*Crime and Punishment* (Dostoevski)	Analytical Reading Direct & Integrated Approaches Style Analysis Notes
WRITING		
16. Write to describe	Photo from "Robo-Legs" article	Three-Column Organizer
17. Write to define	* "Emmanuel Yeboah preps for Fitness Triathlon" * "Walking Off the Fat, Across the Land" * "Find and Focus"	Traits That Contribute to Economic Success Target Notes
18. Write to inform	* "Leaders and Success: Abraham Lincoln"	Main Idea Organizer Organization Patterns Academic Writing
19. Develop a topic	Students' writing	Target Notes Main Idea Organizer
20. Begin an essay	* *Inc.* Magazine's "Most Fascinating Entrepreneurs: Reuben Martinez"	Main Idea Organizer
21. Craft an effective argument	Students' writing	Target Notes Argument Organizer
22. Summarize	Online article	Understanding Arg.: An Overview Summary Notes Conversational Roundtable Summary Exemplar
23. Write an effective paragraph	Students' writing	Summary Exemplar Summary Notes Organizational Patterns Analytical Paragraph Comparison Organizer Main Idea Organizer
24. Paraphrase	* "I Hear America Singing" (Whitman) * "I, Too, Sing America" (Hughes)	Paraphrase Prep

Essential Performance	Text	Tool
25. **Compare and contrast**	* "Facing It" (Komunyakaa) * "Dulce et Decorum Est" (Owens)	Comparison Organizer
26. **Improve academic writing**	*Heart of Darkness* (Conrad)	Analytical Paragraph Analytical Paragraph Samples
27. **Synthesize multiple sources**	*Heart of Darkness* (Conrad) * "Genesis 3: 1-24" * "Vocation" (Stafford) * "What Work Is" (Levine)	Main Idea Organizer
28. **Write a response to literature**	*Crime and Punishment* (Dostoevski)	Analyzing Symbolism Literature Circle Notes: Overview Structured Response Notes
29. **Write about a theme**	*Crime and Punishment* (Dostoevski)	Theme Tool
30. **Write an effective introduction**	Students' writing AP prompt, sample essay	Writing Effective Introductions Introduction Evaluation
SPEAKING AND LISTENING		
31. **Contribute to class discussion**	*Crime and Punishment* (Dostoevski) * "Measure of a Man's Life: As a Criminal" * "Measure of a Man's Life: As a Redeemer"	Summary Response Notes Summary Notes Discussion Cards Article Notes
32. **Participate in small group discussion**	*The Joy Luck Club* (Tan)	Discussion Cards Conversational Roundtable Conv. Roundtable Guidelines Literature Circle Notes Article Notes
33. **Prepare a speech**	Students' topics	Icebreaker Speech Target Notes Speech Prep Notes Elem. of an Eff. Speech or Pres. Speech Evaluation
34. **Make an effective presentation**	Students' topics	Episodic Notes Presentation Slides Elem. of an Eff. Speech or Pres.
35. **Listen and respond to speakers**	Guest speaker's presentation	Speaker Notes Speech Evaluation
TAKING NOTES		
36. **Take notes from expository prose**	* "MySpace Morphs into Phenom"	Conversational Roundtable
37. **Take notes from lectures**	Topic: listening	Teaching Note-Taking Skills Making Effective and Efficient Notes Cornell Notes (Intro) Cornell Notes (Blank) Leonardo da Vinci's Notes
38. **Take notes from literature**	*Lord of the Flies* (Golding)	Literature Circle Notes: Overview Literature Circle Notes: Discussion

cont. on next page

Essential Performance	Text	Tool
38. Take notes from literature (continued)	*Lord of the Flies* (Golding)	Director, Illuminator, Illustrator, Connector, Word Watcher, Summarizer Literature Circle Notes: Illustrator Student Sample Book Notes: Essential Information Lit Notes Character Study Conversational Roundtable
39. Take notes from textbooks	Topic: communication	Making Eff. and Efficient Notes Teaching Note-Taking Skills Textbook Feature Analysis Textbook Notes (Exemplar) Q Notes Interactive Notes
40. Take notes from videos	Video: *Abraham Lincoln: Preserving the Union* (Biography)	Video Notes Interactive Notes Reporter's Notes
TAKING TESTS		
41. Take multiple-choice tests	Exit exam practice text	Test-Taking Strategy Directions Personal Reading Assessment Reflective Reading Quiz Reflective Reading Quiz (Exemplar)
42. Write likely test questions	Students' sustained silent reading (SSR) books	Personal Reading Assessment Test Creator Test Question Creator Test-Maker Tool Dense Question Strategy
43. Learn content for a test	Vocabulary list	Make and Use Study Cards
44. Take essay tests	Classroom essay prompt *To Kill a Mockingbird* (Lee)	Main Idea Organizer
45. Analyze sample essays	AP Lit. prompt, essays, and guidelines	
MANAGING ONESELF		
46. Use a planner	Academic planner	Student Weekly Planner
47. Set goals and plan to reach them	Student's record of goals and progress	Weekly Record Personal Progress Report
48. Study traits of successful people	* "Managing Oneself" * Inc. Magazine's "Most Fascinating Entrepreneurs: Reuben Martinez" Online resources	ACCESS Final Exam
49. Manage your attention	Mel Levine's "Concentration Cockpit"	The Concentration Cockpit
50. Monitor your academic performance	Students' self-assessment	Weekly Record Academic Habits Self-Evaluation Main Idea Organizer Personal Progress Report Finals Preparation Checklist

> *Different students have different strengths, but **every student** needs to achieve an essential mastery of multiple means of communication in order to meet the varied demands of school, life, and workplace. "*

What *are* the **Essential Lessons**, and where do they come from?

EVERY DAY I WALK INTO A CLASSROOM WHERE I TEACH KIDS *from both ends of the continuum—freshmen and seniors, at-risk and advanced, those who read way below grade level and those who read way above—all of whom must meet the rigorous demands of the present and the future. I have large classes and less time in which to teach the same lessons I did before we changed to a new schedule that trimmed eight minutes off each period. In other words, my situation is like most other teachers in the country: I am expected to do a lot, in less time, for all my students, most of whom come in without the skills or knowledge they need to do the work I assign. Writing* 50 Essential Lessons *is the result of the lessons I've learned while asking how to teach my students the skills they need to succeed in my class, our school, and their future. In many respects, this is the most personal of all my books for teachers: it brings you into my classroom, where I have taught every one of these lessons to the kids you see pictured. Thus* 50 Essential Lessons *offers you practical steps based on research, my own as well as others' in the field of adolescent literacy.*

Addressing "Core Standards"

The Essential Lessons are, foremost, anchored in standards taken from a range of national literacy standards found in both secondary- and post-secondary-level documents. This is, above all, the world in which we now teach, one far removed from when I entered the profession in 1989 and, when I asked what I had to teach, was given nothing but a sheet of paper with the titles of some books. While some resist the push for standards, I welcome it as an effort to achieve greater social equity for all and provide improved support to teachers entering the classroom for the first time. I have deliberately chosen what some districts call "power standards" or "core standards," as these tend to represent not just what the state exams assess but also what such tests as the AP, ACT, and SAT expect students to know. Moreover, universities have become much more vocal about what they expect students to know upon arrival, so

I have consulted a range of reports (Conley, 2005; Educational Testing Service, 2003; Intersegmental Committees of the Academic Senates, 2002) to cull from them those "academic essentials" students must have to gain entrance to and succeed in college.

Many of the increased expectations for my students came not from my own district but rather from the California superintendent of public instruction himself (O'Connell, 2004); these higher expectations are increasingly the rule, not the exception (Maxwell, 2006). My school district, in an effort to provide a rigorous curriculum, adopted the state university entrance requirements as our own graduation requirements for all students.

In addition, several organizations (Achieve, 2004; ACT/Education Trust, 2005; Alliance for Excellence in Education, 2004; ETS, 2003; WestEd, 2005), through both political and public campaigns, are joining forces to advocate for high standards as a means of ensuring that all students have access to a college-preparatory education. All these initiatives leave teachers feeling unprecedented pressure about how to teach the necessary skills so that all students can learn and use them to gain access to further educational opportunities.

> *All these initiatives leave teachers feeling unprecedented pressure about how to teach the necessary skills so that all students can learn.... Thus one of the essential lessons we all learn is how to juggle many balls at once.*

50 Essential Lessons derives from these different standards documents, but I do not pretend to offer here a complete curriculum that addresses all the major English Language Arts standards. A quick glance at the table of contents, for example, finds no direct mention of either grammar or vocabulary. While these are surely essential components of the English Language Arts curriculum, I chose to focus on more generative aspects of the curriculum, particularly those elements that will promote success in *all* core academic subject areas. You will see, for example, many instances where, in the context of the lessons, I help students acquire academic vocabulary, that is, vocabulary that will engender student success across disciplines. After all, one of the greatest challenges we face, aside from providing a curriculum that is personally meaningful to all students in our classes, is to fit in everything we are charged with teaching. Thus one of the essential lessons we all learn is how to juggle many balls at once, how to embrace and eventually master the simultaneity of teaching everything we must to everyone we teach (Lampert, 2001).

Solutions to Instructional Problems

Teaching, Not Assigning

While the lessons address standards, they are also solutions to the instructional problems we face in trying to teach students *how*, for example, to analyze an author's argument or examine multiple perspectives. As readers and writers ourselves, we demonstrate these abilities reflexively, our minds whirring like operating systems in the background to execute the necessary commands we learned so long ago that they are now just second nature. Our students need us to make these processes *visible*.

These lessons are about teaching, not assigning; moreover, they are about how and what we need to learn as teachers so that we can be consistently effective in our instruction. As the structure of these lessons evolved, I learned to be more deliberate when planning and teaching. Creating the lessons forced me to ask such questions as

"What must my students know and be able to do to complete this task or learn this technique I want to teach them?" Instead of assuming my students show up knowing how to do what I assign, I have learned to see school as a place where kids need to *learn how* to do what we assign. When they already are able to complete a task successfully, I have learned to extend my planned lessons and to move beyond what they already know and are able to do. For even at the most advanced levels, we should be asking students to work beyond the standards (Jago, 2001).

Personal Professional Development

50 Essential Lessons also provides an opportunity for personal professional development, something we all need but that our schools struggle to find time to provide us. The lessons offered here reflect many elements of "lesson study" (Stigler and Hiebert, 1999), which begins with the premise that "if you want to improve teaching, the most effective place to do so is in the context of a classroom lesson" (p. 110). The lesson study process, outlined in *The Teaching Gap*, identifies eight steps (p. 113) that guided my work:

1. **Define** the problem.
2. **Plan** the lesson.
3. **Teach** the lesson.
4. **Evaluate** the lesson and **reflect** on its effect.
5. **Revise** the lesson.
6. **Teach** the revised lesson.
7. **Evaluate** and **reflect**—again.
8. **Share** the results.

No one will learn more from these lessons than I did by writing them, analyzing my own techniques, and studying my craft, but the results of my lesson study are in your hands, allowing you, I hope, time to focus on the steps, above. For through the process of identifying, planning, teaching, evaluating, revising, (re)teaching, and reflecting, we take responsibility for our own professional development instead of waiting to see what the district, the school, or our department will provide to help us solve the instructional problems we face daily.

"Academic Essentials"

In addition to examining my own instructional methods while teaching and writing *50 Essential Lessons*, I continued to analyze, as I have in my recent books, the academic demands common to all classes. The result of this analysis is what I call the "Academic Essentials" (Burke, 2005, p. 78). A glance at the table of contents of *50 Essential Lessons* shows that the Academic Essentials (see Figure 1.1, following page) form the overarching structure of the program offered here. The Academic Essentials are further stressed and visible in the "Assess and Extend" section at the end of each lesson. While the Academic Essentials themselves are my own construction, the idea draws on past efforts to identify those skills common to all academic classes (Bloom, 1956; Costa, 2001; Costa and Ballick, 2000; Marzano, 2001; Marzano, Pickering, and Pollock, 2001; Pauk, 1997; Rose, 1989). The Academic Essentials continue to provide me with a guide during planning and teaching, reminding me of what I must accomplish and how I might extend and thus improve the instructional effectiveness of the lessons I teach.

In *ACCESSing School* (Burke, 2005), I offer the following summary of what the Academic Essentials (AE) matrix is and how I use it:

> The AE matrix gives structure, depth, and sequencing to my lessons. For example, when I decide which of the "Skills" (reading, writing, talking, taking notes, or taking tests) I need to focus on next, I then use the "Abilities" to organize and improve that instruction. If we are reading an article on the topic of personal success, for example, I might have students "generate" a list of factors they think contribute to such success. I might then have students, to increase their processing of the information, "evaluate" which *three* factors from their list are the most important and then "analyze" how they contribute to success. The matrix challenges me to achieve more but in a structured sequence; thus I might have students "organize" their three essential factors from most to least important or in some other logical order. Finally, to integrate the different skills,

Figure 1.1
Academic Essentials

SKILLS		Generate (Questions, Hypotheses, Claims, Explanations, Examples)	Evaluate (Importance, Effectiveness, Relevance, Validity, Accuracy)	Analyze (Cause-Effect, Meaning, Implications, Logic, Consequences)	Organize (Events, Information, Process, Ideas, Emphasis)	Synthesize (Information, Events, Ideas, Sources, Perspectives)
Read	• Fiction • Information • Argument • Poetry					
Write	• Reader Response • Narrative • Expository • Argument					
Talk	• Discussion • Speech • Presentation					
Take Notes	• Expository • Research • Literary • Textbook					
Take Tests	• Multiple-Choice • Essay • Short-Answer • Standardized					

I would have students "synthesize" by first writing a well-organized paragraph and then, if time allows, discussing it with each other or the class. In addition, I would ask myself (before, during, and after this instructional sequence) what other skills—writing, talking, taking notes, taking tests—I could or should integrate. In this way, the AE matrix ensures my instruction is designed to achieve maximum effectiveness in ways that promote learning and academic success.

Since developing this matrix, I have added a sixth "essential": managing oneself. You will find a cluster of lessons focused on managing oneself in the table of contents.

The Classroom Context

Ultimately, the lessons detailed here come from my daily firsthand experience as a public high school teacher. For that reason, it seems appropriate to describe the context in which these lessons were taught, the students with whom I work, and the conditions under which I taught these particular lessons. I currently teach two classes: AP English Literature and ACCESS, which is an acronym for Academic Success. Both classes are larger than they should be: thirty-five in the AP classes and, the year during which I wrote *50 Essential Lessons*, twenty-eight in the ACCESS class. The rigors of AP Lit are well known, but the nature of the class is changing in my own school and many others. What was, just a few years ago, a course offered only to an "elite" corps of students has, in many schools around the country, become open to anyone who wants to take it. This "open-enrollment policy" means that roughly fifty percent of the seniors at my high school enroll in AP Literature, yet only about twenty-five percent of them enter with the intellectual skills and rigor common to the classes in the past. So I have to teach them much more about *how* to read, write, and talk about such sophisticated texts as *Hamlet* and *Crime and Punishment* or the poetry of Yeats than I expected when I began teaching the course. In short, I quickly realized that despite being in an AP class, the majority of the students were not much different from those in my ACCESS class, in that they were struggling to read, write, and think at the expected levels and needed help learning to do so.

I have written about ACCESS in great detail in *ACCESSing School: Teaching Struggling Readers to Achieve Academic and Personal Success* (Heinemann, 2005). It is, foremost, a reading class, one students are assigned to take if they come in reading two or more grade levels below the ninth grade. It is not a remedial English or Special Education class, but it exists to help them succeed in their mainstream academic classes such as English, Contemporary World Studies, Health, and, to a lesser extent, World Languages and Biology. Sitting at the center of their academic wheel, I see all that they are expected to be able to do in these other classes and I help them learn the academic essentials and develop the academic vocabulary needed to succeed. It is through the ACCESS class that I identified what I referred to, above, as the "Academic Essentials." Yet these essentials are not limited to the ACCESS students; indeed, a quick survey of what my AP students had to do in high school and college proved these were the same cognitive and personal skills they would need to succeed after they graduated, too.

Finally, I must briefly explain the conditions under which I taught the lessons included in this book, for they are an important factor. In previous years, I had grown somewhat used to having access to technology in my classroom and making effective use of it to enrich or improve my instruction. In the last two years, however, the time during which I developed these lessons, I worked in a sparse environment: a portable classroom with an overhead projector and a whiteboard. While I believe technology offers important benefits, working without it—having just the basics—was liberating: paper, whiteboard, overhead projector, and ink are things most teachers have in one form or another in their classrooms. So the lessons here do not make any assumptions about advanced technology or resources. Moreover, I had less time than ever before: fifty minutes per class. Our school had just shifted to a seven-period schedule, which translated to a loss of eight minutes per period. Thus I had to learn to work with maximum efficiency within strict constraints of time and resources. In the end, these constraints provided an "invitation to struggle," which led to the instructional process outlined in *50 Essential Lessons*.

> *...The lessons here do not make any assumptions about advanced technology or resources.*

The photographs in the lessons show my students—either in my portable or in my old classroom—doing whatever it is I am describing in the lesson. My method for these photographs is very simple: I keep a camera in my pocket and capture on the fly what good work looks like. The photographs of me were taken by my student aides and so are also authentic.

How to Use the Essential Lessons

Perhaps I can answer the question "What are the 'Essential Lessons'?" best by saying what they are *not*. They are not a collection of scripts or recipes for you to follow word-for-word so that you sound and act like me. I see them instead as a means of helping you discover and develop your own voice by studying mine. The first thing one learns as a new teacher is how hard it is to teach "someone else's stuff," for we must, in the end, make their ideas our own. While I am confident that you can use any of these fifty lessons and the corresponding tools tomorrow with whatever and whomever you are teaching, I am also confident that you can adopt and adapt what you find within my lessons to help you craft your own lessons that meet your students' individual needs. In *Tools and Texts,* you will find a Lesson Planning Tool—a template for you to use to do just that. It is my hope that through these essential lessons, all our students will graduate prepared to learn and apply the essential *life* lessons that await them as citizens, employees, parents, and lifelong students.

> "By reflecting on our teaching we develop, as athletes do after watching the game tapes, a deeper understanding of our 'moves'... and become more fluent, more cognizant, and thus more effective."

What are the guiding principles in my teaching and the Essential Lessons?

As I wrote *50 Essential Lessons* and analyzed my teaching, *I looked for common threads, principles that inform what I do, how I do it, and why. These principles, the more I became aware of them, improved my own teaching because they made me aware of what I did that made a difference. While I offer them here to provide a theoretical foundation for the lessons, I also encourage you to use my principles to reflect on yours. By reflecting on our teaching, we develop, as athletes do after watching the game tapes, a deeper understanding of our "moves" in different situations, and through that increased awareness, we become more fluent, more cognizant, and thus more effective (Hillocks, 2005). After much reflection, I have identified the following ten principles as the core of the Essential Lessons.*

Effective instruction, as I will explain in detail further on, teaches students how to:

1. Work independently and with others to solve a range of intellectual problems.
2. Process material on multiple levels and in various ways.
3. Use tools and strategies to solve a range of academic problems.
4. Learn skills and knowledge through a range of instructional modes.
5. Communicate understanding by multiple means, including different media.
6. Monitor and evaluate personal performance and progress toward goals.
7. Connect what is learned today to self, other studies, and the world.
8. Develop and use skills and knowledge in the context of meaningful conversations.
9. Know what a successful performance looks like on all tasks and assessments.
10. Read a variety of types of texts, including multimedia and visual.

Work independently and with others to solve a range of intellectual problems.

The world expects students to be able to work independently as well as with others (Olson, 2006). Group work, however, must have structure and purpose in order to improve engagement, comprehension, and memory (Angelis, 2003; Langer, 2000; Langer and Close, 2001; Marzano, 2001; National Council of Teachers of English, 2006; Zemelman, Daniels, and Hyde, 2005). Such collaboration offers additional support for English language learners (Echevarria and Graves, 2003; NCTE, 2006) and those with special needs, giving the teacher a way to differentiate instruction (Tomlinson, 1999) so that these students can hear how others discuss a particular problem and see how they work to solve it. Working together to solve problems is an essential life skill for all students. Frequent group work helps students develop skills that also help them work more effectively alone.

Students must be able to work independently in a variety of contexts. They may enjoy working in "lit circles" on a novel, but they don't get to do that on the state or AP tests; thus they must be able to show the world that they can do on their own what they can do in a group.

In *The English Teacher's Companion* (Burke, 2003), I use the term "Continuum of Performance" to represent this movement from dependence to independence and back again. All of us (students, teachers, readers, writers, and thinkers) continually move back and forth along this continuum as we learn and, over time, improve. Such movement signals improved fluency as students learn to perform increasingly complex tasks on their own by using those strategies that help them progress from where they are to where they need to be academically (Alliance for Education, 2004; Vygotsky, 1978). The following sequence, which I use in various lessons, illustrates such a progression. In this sequence, students progress from working independently to working with a group. In other lessons, students begin in groups and then later work on their own. Both variations are useful.

▶ **Working Alone**

- *Generate* a list of words that you could use to describe a character.
- *Evaluate* those words and choose the one you think *best* describes him or her.
- *Analyze* and note how that word applies to the character.
- *Organize* your details according to some principle such as order of importance.
- *Synthesize* your ideas by writing a brief character analysis.

▶ **Working with Others**

- *Share* your words with the group, generating a second list.
- *Evaluate* all the words in your group and decide which one out of them all is the *best* word for this character.
- *Analyze* how that word applies to the character, generating examples and details to support and illustrate your point.

- ***Synthesize*** everyone's ideas by moving into a full class discussion, during which each group shares its words, the teacher puts them on the board, and everyone evaluates all the words to find one word the whole class agrees is the best word to describe the character.

- For homework, use your notes to ***write*** a more formal character analysis with supporting details from the text; bring your analysis in the next day.

Note how, aside from being built around the academic essential verbs—synthesize, analyze, evaluate, generate, organize—each stage prepares the student for the stage that follows, in this case sending students to their groups ready to share their words while at the same time providing them with an opportunity to see how others solved the same problem. Such text-based collaborative learning, when anchored in discussion (Alliance for Excellent Education, 2004; Applebee, Langer, Nystrand, and Gamoran, 2003; Langer and Close, 2001), fosters a lively community within the class while also developing skills and knowledge that lead to improved performance on other tasks, including tests, since sequences such as the one above integrate test preparation, in this case, analytical writing practice, into a larger, more meaningful curricular discussion (Applebee, 1999; Langer, 2000).

I tend to think of this process as a cycle that can potentially begin and end fruitfully at multiple points. (See Figure 1.2.) If it is robust, this cycle, or continuum, leads to the next principle: active processing.

Figure 1.2
Continuum of Performance

2   *Process material on multiple levels and in various ways.*

The best, most delicious way to understand this principle is to think about the process of making a pizza. You knead the dough, stretching and pulling, twisting and flinging as you work in the different elements that will make it rise; then you start building it up, layer after layer, adding one thing to another, each topping meant to complement the others. Then you bake it, turning everything into one delicious, brilliant pie of complex understanding. In other words, kids need to take the material in hand—whether it's a poem, a problem, or a concept—and "mess about" with it, moving through successive levels of complexity that require "guided inquiry," all of which lead to a "culminating performance" (Ritchhart, et al., 1998) that they can only do well if they have processed the material to such an extent that they have "internalized it" and thus made the material their own (Vygotsky, 1978).

> *Kids need to take the material in hand—whether it's a poem, a problem, or a concept—and "mess about" with it, moving through successive levels of complexity.*

Researchers (Beuhl, 2001; Clarke, 1990) find it is just such robust, deep processing that leads to improved understanding, fluency, and memory, all of which result in improved performance in those areas the lessons address. It is the work of Robert Marzano that informs my thinking most profoundly here. In his book *Designing a New Taxonomy of Educational Objectives* (2001), Marzano offers a new angle on the work begun by Benjamin Bloom (1956), organizing knowledge into domains and thinking into systems, using his "new taxonomy" to show how teachers can consistently move students beyond mere "retrieval" and "comprehension" into more advanced levels such as analysis and utilization. (See Figure 1.3, following page.)

OBJECTIVES	DESCRIPTION
for the **Levels of Marzano's New Taxonomy**	
Level 6: Self-System Examining Importance Examining Efficacy Examining Emotional Response Examining Motivation	**Beliefs and goals used to make judgments about engaging in a new task.** • Identifies how important the knowledge is and reasoning underlying this perception. • Identifies beliefs about ability to improve ability or understanding related to knowledge. • Identifies emotional responses to knowledge and reasons for these responses. • Identifies own level of motivation to improve competence or understanding.
Level 5: Metacognition Goal Specification Process Monitoring Monitoring Clarity Monitoring Accuracy	**Sets goals relative to new task; designs strategies to accomplish this goal.** • Sets a plan for goals relative to the knowledge. • Monitors the execution of knowledge. • Determines the extent to which he/she has clarity about the knowledge. • Determines the extent to which he/she is accurate about the knowledge.
Level 4: Utilization Decision Making Problem Solving Experimental Inquiry Investigation	**Processes someone uses to accomplish a specific task.** • Uses the knowledge to make decisions or makes decisions about the uses of knowledge. • Uses the knowledge to solve problems or solves problems about the knowledge. • Uses the knowledge to generate and test hypotheses or generates and tests hypotheses about the knowledge. • Uses the knowledge to conduct investigations or conducts investigations about the knowledge.
Level 3: Analysis Matching Classifying Error Analysis Generalizing Specifying	**Involves the generation of new information not already possessed by individual.** • Identifies important similarities and differences between types of knowledge. • Identifies superordinate and subordinate categories related to knowledge. • Identifies errors in presentation or use of knowledge. • Constructs new generalizations or principles based on knowledge. • Identifies specific applications or logical consequences of knowledge.
Level 2: Comprehension Synthesis Representation	**Translates knowledge into a form appropriate for storage in permanent memory.** • Identifies the basic structure of knowledge and the critical as opposed to noncritical characteristics. • Accurately represents in nonlinguistic or symbolic form the basic structure of knowledge and the critical as opposed to noncritical aspects.
Level 1: Retrieval Recall Execution	**The activation and transfer of knowledge from permanent to working memory.** • Can identify or recognize features of info but does not necessarily understand the structure of knowledge or differentiate critical from noncritical components. • Can perform a procedure without significant error but does not necessarily understand how and why the procedure works.

Figure 1.3
**Objectives for Marzano's
New Taxonomy**

"Objectives for the Levels of Marzano's New Taxonomy Description" from *Designing a New Taxonomy of Educational Objectives* ed. by T. R. Guskey and R. J. Marzano. Copyright © 2001 Corwin Press. Reprinted by permission of Corwin Press.

Implementing Marzano's ideas creates a much more interactive environment, one that accelerates and deepens learning by all students, including English language learners (Chamot and O'Mally, 1994), who are likely to begin on the more literal level and, through successive interactions, arrive at a more conceptual understanding, which enables them to apply the material to other situations. The goal is to provide multiple "entry points" into the material, allowing students at all levels to begin where they are and, through these different cognitive processes, reach new levels (Gardner, 1999; Tomlinson, 1999). Langer (2001) found that students who are taught and expected to be "generative thinkers" achieve sustained, significant gains in their reading and writing performance; subsequent studies (Langer and Close, 2001; Nystrand, 2006) concluded that using discussion in various structured ways leads to further gains in reading comprehension. Langer identifies other "generative" activities, such as having students:

- *Explore* texts from many points of view (e.g., social, historical, ethical, political, personal).
- *Extend* literary understanding beyond initial interpretations.
- *Research* and *discuss* issues generated by literary texts and by student concerns.
- *Extend* research questions beyond their original focus.
- *Develop* ideas in writing that go beyond the superficial.
- *Write* from different points of view.
- *Design* follow-up lessons that cause students to move beyond their initial thinking.

One last means of processing information is to use tools such as graphic organizers; these are the subjects of the next principle, which will explore their use in more detail.

3 Use tools and strategies to solve a range of academic problems.

What some call "visual tools" (Hyerle, 1996), "nonlinguistic representations" (Marzano, 2001), or "graphic organizers" (Beyer, 2001; Clarke, 1990), I call "tools for thought" (Burke, 2002). I prefer to call them tools because that is how we use them in my class; we also use them to do much more than merely "organize" or "represent." We use them to help us learn and do all of the "academic essentials": read, write, speak, take notes, take tests, and manage oneself (mirroring the traditional academic verbs: generate, evaluate, analyze, organize, and synthesize). Hyerle (1996), summing up years of research findings, notes that these "visual tools" enhance the following:

- Motivation to learn
- Basic skills of reading, writing, and arithmetic
- Content knowledge retention
- General communication skills
- Organizing abilities
- Independent and cooperative learning

- Problem-solving flexibility
- Creative and analytical thinking
- Conceptual understandings
- Higher-order thinking
- Metacognitive abilities and self-assessment
- Enjoyment of problem solving

I first explored the use of tools in my English class when I found myself teaching five sophomore English classes, each with approximately thirty-five students, many of whom were "transitional English language learners" (ready to study in the mainstream). Faced with such a wide range of needs and abilities in a large class, I realized that my students needed to learn a range of strategies (Alliance for Excellence in Education, 2004; Langer, 1999; National Council of Teachers of English, 2006) and that these tools could help them do that, giving them the structure they would need to solve the various academic problems encountered in my class. Since that time, regardless of the level of need of the students, I have become a much more visual teacher, realizing in the process that thought has *a shape to it* and tools can help students better understand and convey their ideas whether in writing, speaking, or representing. The "shape" of thought often accords with the different rhetorical modes or "text frames" (Buehl, 2001), thus allowing me to choose, as my father taught me long ago, "the right tool for the job." If, for example, we are going to compare and contrast two or more texts, we might use Comparison Notes or the Main Idea Organizer; should we want to develop a persuasive essay or speech, we would use the Argument Organizer.

A completed Conversational Roundtable, for example, is a beginning, preparing students for what is the real work of the day: reading, writing, or speaking.

It is too easy to see a completed tool as an end result, but effective use of these tools means, of course, going beyond that. A completed Conversational Roundtable, for example, is a beginning, preparing students for what is the real work of the day: reading, writing, or speaking. I frequently remind myself not to overuse tools and never to turn them into busywork or default solutions. When you use them, I recommend that you always try them first yourself. Then model their use—on the overhead, whiteboard, or butcher paper—for students as you are setting up the assignment.

All the tools are located in *Tools and Texts* and on the accompanying CD-ROM. Throughout the lessons you will see facsimiles of the tools at their point of use, in the context of teaching sequences. A representative sequence might begin by having students read a batch of sonnets for homework and then come to class to find a copy of the Conversational Roundtable on the overhead. I will begin by telling them what I want them to do in groups; then I will model for them how to use the tool in their groups to accomplish this end. Each student will complete the same tool through collaborative discussion, which prepares them for the next stage: using their notes to write a well-organized piece of analytical prose. The tool, due to its structure, will have effectively prepared them for this task by having them generate categories, details, and quotations, all related to the subject at the center of the tool. Such a sequence illustrates the next principle about instructional modes.

4. Learn skills and knowledge through a range of instructional modes.

The more I study and write about adolescent literacy, the more I come to see one central subject running throughout: teaching so that students can learn. I can ingest all the content I am able to, but unless I find techniques I can use to *teach* that content—whether a skill or a fact—to each student in my class, we have all lost. Given today's diverse classrooms, teachers must use multiple entry points (Gardner, 1999) to increase the likelihood of motivating all kids to learn the skills and knowledge necessary to what Gardner calls a "disciplined mind." Tapping into kids' multiple intelligences, teachers can use any or all of the following instructional entry points: narrative, numerical, logical, existential/foundational, aesthetic, hands-on, or interpersonal (Gardner, 1992, 1999).

Tomlinson offers, through her model of "differentiated instruction," an alternative but complementary approach. She argues that teachers can respond to each learner's needs by providing "respectful tasks, flexible grouping, and ongoing assessment and adjustment" (1999). She suggests that teachers can use different modes according to students' needs, differentiating three specific components of their instruction: the content students learn, the process they will use to learn it, or the product by which they will demonstrate they have learned the lesson. Which path the teacher follows

COMPARING CLASSROOMS	
TRADITIONAL CLASSROOM	**DIFFERENTIATED CLASSROOM**
• Student differences are masked or acted upon when problematic.	• Student differences are studied as a basis for planning.
• Assessment is most common at the end of learning to see "who got it."	• Assessment is ongoing and diagnostic to understand how to make instruction more responsive to learner need.
• A relatively narrow sense of intelligence prevails.	• Focus on multiple forms of intelligences is evident.
• A single definition of excellence exists.	• Excellence is defined in large measure by individual growth from a starting point.
• Student interest is infrequently tapped.	• Students are frequently guided in making interest-based learning choices.
• Relatively few learning profile options are taken into account.	• Many learning profile options are provided for.
• Whole-class instruction dominates.	• Many instructional arrangements are used.
• Coverage of texts and curriculum guides drives instruction.	• Student readiness, interest, and learning profile shape instruction.
• Mastery of facts and skills out-of-context are the focus of learning.	• Use of essential skills to make sense of and understand key concepts and principles is the focus of learning.
• Single option assignments are the norm.	• Multi-option assignments are frequently used.
• Time is relatively inflexible.	• Time is used flexibly in accordance with student need.
• A single text prevails.	• Multiple materials are provided.
• Single interpretations of ideas and events may be sought.	• Multiple perspectives on ideas and events are routinely sought.
• The teacher directs student behavior.	• The teacher facilitates students' skills at becoming more self-reliant learners.
• The teacher solves problems.	• Students help other students and the teacher solve problems.
• The teacher provides whole-class standards for grading.	• Students work with the teacher to establish both whole-class and individual learning goals.
• A single form of assessment is often used.	• Students are assessed in multiple ways.

Figure 1.4
Comparing Classrooms

From "The Differentiated Classroom: Responding to the Needs of All Learners" by Carol Ann Tomlinson. Alexandria, VA: ASCD, 1999.

depends on each student's individual readiness, interests, and learning profile. Tomilson compares the "traditional" and "differentiated" classroom in Figure 1.4, above, giving us a concise look at what it means to use a variety of instructional modes.

Using "multiple lesson types" allows teachers to be more effective, giving them a means by which to assess not only what the student must actually learn but also how he or she can best learn it. Langer (1999) reflects Tomlinson's use of different "processes" to teach skills and knowledge but offers a more succinct model of three "lesson types" or "activities": separated, simulated, and integrated. *Separated* activities are appropriate for isolated skills, rules, or details one might need to know to complete subsequent, more complex tasks. *Simulated* activities, which allow students to practice and apply their skills and knowledge, require students to, for example, identify and analyze the author's use of imagery while reading a literary work, thus extending the *separated* lessons. *Integrated* activities, Langer's third lesson type, allow students to learn what they need as they solve a series of intellectual problems as part of a more complex assignment or project. Advocates of project-based learning (PBL) emphasize this approach as the most important mode of instruction, pointing out that PBL develops and reflects the "21st century skills" needed in a rapidly changing workplace (Partnership for 21st Century Skills, 2006; Pearlman, 2006). Many of my model lessons were created to help my students learn skills they needed as part of a complex task or project, such as giving a speech, learning to be successful in life, or preparing for a high-stakes test. The "Assess and Extend" section that concludes each lesson provides multiple ideas for differentiating and extending instruction based on your students' needs.

5 Communicate understanding by multiple means, including different media.

In a world saturated by media—text messaging, the Internet, and downloading of images—students must learn to communicate ideas in the most appropriate medium by the most effective means. I have referred to this ability to communicate effectively in multiple mediums as "textual intelligence" (Burke, 2001), arguing that in a world full of competing means of communication, the workplace will demand that students be able to read and produce messages in different media for different audiences and distribute their messages by increasingly diverse means—the most recent of which is the podcast. For example, one man I know is currently producing interactive travel guides that will incorporate video, images, and text and be made available through cell phones; thus he must consider not only how to convey his content but also how people will *use* (as opposed to merely read) his multimedia text.

How students choose to convey their ideas should ultimately depend on the context and purpose of the communication. Given access to necessary technology, students should be encouraged and even required, at times, to use technology to communicate their understanding, for it is the lack of essential technology skills that most consistently stands as a barrier between lower-income students and their more affluent, connected peers (National Council of Teachers of English, 2006) when they all enter the workforce where a global economy demands global skills (Friedman, 2005).

While it is important to give students the opportunity to express themselves by whatever means or medium helps them succeed, these mediums cannot replace the teaching and learning of primary means of communicating: reading, writing, speaking, and taking tests. All students must master these at some level. Throughout all fifty lessons, I never forget that at some point students will be expected—by the state, the College Board, college professors, or even the workplace—to, for example, write in clear, effective prose that follows the conventions of good writing.

Different students have different strengths, but every student needs to achieve an essential mastery of multiple means of communication in order to meet the varied demands of school, life, and workplace.

The *50 Essential Lessons* table of contents is, in fact, organized in the following clusters: Reading, Writing, Speaking and Listening, Taking Notes, Taking Tests, and Managing Oneself. Within these clusters, you will find lessons, such as "Make an Effective Presentation" (Lesson 34) and "Examine Multiple Perspectives" (Lesson 10), and ideas in "Assess and Extend" sections that provide opportunities for students to develop these "primary" means of communication *and* enhance their ability to communicate through technology.

Different students have different strengths, but every student needs to achieve an essential mastery of multiple means of communication in order to meet the varied demands of school, life, and workplace.

6 *Monitor and evaluate personal performance and progress toward goals.*

I teach classes that culminate in precise scores that measure my students'—and *my*—performance against their classmates and against national norms. In my AP English Literature class, we are all aware that one day in the first week of May they will wake up, gulp down some breakfast, and rush to school, where they will sit down and take a three-hour exam that assesses the knowledge and skills we have worked all year to develop.

My students periodically take standardized reading tests—the Gates-McGinitie and the Scholastic Reading Inventory—to measure their progress as readers; in addition to these tests, they will take the district "common assessment" in key academic disciplines and, come April, the state exam, which is aligned with all the state standards. If I were teaching sophomores, I would be reminded routinely that come March they must take the state exit exam for the first time, and if I taught juniors, I would be constantly aware of the new SAT exam and how it aligns with my English curriculum, particularly in the areas of language study and writing. A new test has just been added to this barrage of assessments for California students: those planning to attend a state university must pass the English Placement Test (EPT). Even if they have been accepted, they will not be allowed to enroll if they do not pass this test and its companion exam in mathematics.

> *The question we all face, in such a climate of summative assessment, is how to teach in ways that develop skills and knowledge without surrendering the meaning, the substance of the course for which we have a passion.*

The question teachers all face, in such a climate of summative assessment, is how to teach in ways that develop skills and knowledge without surrendering the meaning, the substance of the course for which we have a passion. First, we must use assessment in ways that result in improved learning and achievement. In her five-year study of effective literacy instruction, Langer (1999) found that those schools that "beat the odds" consistently "integrate test preparation into instruction." Her report identifies several activities that work, such as having teachers:

- Analyze the demands of a test.
- Identify connections to the standards and goals.
- Design and align curriculum to meet the demands of the test.
- Develop instructional strategies that enable students to build the necessary skills.
- Ensure that skills are learned across the year and across grades.
- Make overt connections between and among instructional strategies, tests, and current learning.
- Develop and implement model lessons that integrate test preparation into the curriculum.

If you skim the table of contents, you will find five lessons under the Taking Tests cluster specifically designed to help you incorporate the activities that Langer outlines above into your classroom instruction.

Equally important is using a variety of types of assessments. In its policy research brief, the National Council of Teachers of English (NCTE) emphasizes that "both teachers and students benefit from multiple forms of evaluation … [since] high-stakes tests rarely provide feedback that has instructional value" (NCTE, 2006, p. 7). The NCTE identifies three types of assessments teachers can use to monitor and evaluate progress:

- *Ongoing formative assessment:* Assessment that provides regular feedback about student learning…enhances motivation as well as achievement….Teachers who receive daily or weekly information about student development can intervene effectively.

- *Informal assessment:* [Examples include] brief responses to a student journal, students' written summaries of learning at the end of class, or a student-teacher conference [that does not] require a grade but provides formative evaluation of student achievement.

- *Formal assessment:* The test at the end of the unit or paper written in response to a multi-week assignment is an example of formal assessment that is usually graded and can be described as summative rather than formative. When prepared and graded by a teacher as part of ongoing instruction, formal assessment can provide useful insights into student learning.

Throughout the lessons themselves and within the additional ideas offered in each lesson's "Assess and Extend" section, you will find multiple examples and modeling of the three kinds of assessment listed above.

The NCTE's findings are consistent with instructional "best practices" (Zemelman, Daniels, and Hyde, 2005) and the findings of the National Research Council (2000), which concluded, "Assessment and feedback are crucial for helping people learn." Assessment that is consistent with principles of effective instruction should:

- Mirror good instruction.

- Happen continuously, but not intrusively, as a part of instruction.

- Provide information (to teachers, students, and parents) about the levels of understanding that students are reaching (NRC, 2000, p. 244).

While I have emphasized here the role of assessment from various perspectives, these perspectives have focused on what the teacher does. Throughout the lessons, you will also see students monitoring their own progress as readers and evaluating their own performance and their classmates' performance as speakers and writers, using a variety of tools and techniques, some of which I created and others that come from the state or such agencies as the College Board.

In the end, we must all—teachers and students—be able to effectively monitor our own performance in relation to performance goals.

In the end, we must all—teachers and students—be able to effectively monitor our own performance in relation to performance goals that our teachers or employers expect us to internalize. For example, my brother-in-law, who works at FedEx, is constantly evaluated according to a range of performance goals; thus he must monitor his own performance in those areas essential to his continuing success. The firefighter and the police officer who came to speak to my classes both stressed the standards they are routinely measured against and that they work hard to meet.

Teaching the lessons themselves is my most demanding means of monitoring and evaluating my own teaching, as I must continually ask myself: Is what I am teaching important? Is my instruction effective? And, most important, are my students learning it in those ways that matter most to me, to themselves, and to the world for which they are preparing themselves? These are my essential questions.

7 Connect what is learned today to self, other studies, and the world.

Students need to do what literate adults do when we read or learn about new subjects: ask what we already know that can help us learn and understand this new material and ask how it relates to what we have studied already or how it connects to our own interests. Unfortunately, what is—in the mind of the teacher—a thrilling new piece of the larger narrative of, for example, the westward expansion that created the nation we love so much, often seems to be dreadfully boring material to many students. In other words, while we may connect the facts in the dull textbook to the historical narrative in our head—which somehow further reinforces the connection to our own personal fascination with our country, its story, and its place in the world—our students may not. Without a network of connections, the facts become overwhelming, dull, and meaningless. The content then represents nothing more to the student than questions on a test, otherwise useless information that must be memorized for a passing grade.

Without a network of connections, the facts become overwhelming, dull, and meaningless.

Stories are so much more interesting than texts. So what are we to do when our students read an informational text that refers to historical events, or a literary text that alludes to Cain and Abel, or to an "LP," which my Bible-illiterate, CD-listening, iPod-generation students have never heard of? We speak often of the value of "visualizing" what we read, but if the text you want to turn into a "movie in your head" is made up of words and subjects you don't know, it's going to be impossible to visualize. Teaching students how to make connections is thus essential, as this skill allows students to access whatever background knowledge they *do* have. Accessing background knowledge is a strategy that successful students and effective readers use automatically; it is my job to make the strategy visible to students who can't (Burke, 2004; Hirsch, 2006; Keene and Zimmerman, 1997; Marzano, 2004). Too often, teachers assume this is an innate skill, no doubt because we, as advanced readers, do it so reflexively, so invisibly, ourselves.

Throughout the lessons, you will see my students and me working hard to make such connections and, in some cases, learning *how* to make them. Making connections, while important for all students, is crucial for struggling students who consistently wonder why they need to learn what we teach. Thus you will see me not only teaching them to connect what they are doing to what they have already learned but also making connections to the world of work and their experience, including their culture. If I am going to bring in an article about a successful person for my students, for example, I will try to find one about a Latino such as Rueben Martinez (named one of *Inc.* magazine's most fascinating entrepreneurs), because I have many Latino students, some of whom question the value of academic learning. Such connections increase motivation and improve commitment (Burke, 2004, 2005) while also deepening understanding as we explore more complex connections.

In my English classes, you will see my students and me bringing in art and related information from the fields of history and philosophy to extend our understanding. In a recent class, while reading Kafka's *Metamorphosis*, we turned to Expressionist painters Otto Dix and Wassily Kandinsky to help us understand the larger context of how artists, including Kafka, were responding to their changing world; to extend that understanding, we examined philosophical writings by Camus (1991) on the Absurd and an excerpt by Watson (2001) on the emerging modern world to which Kafka was reacting, including developments in science and business.

Such a cluster of connections turns the class itself into a text, one woven of many strands into a more complex, interesting fabric that emphasizes the importance of the curriculum as a *conversation* (Applebee, 1996; Burke, 2003) not just about skills but about *ideas*. Langer (2001) confirms the importance of "making connections across instruction, curriculum, grades, and life," identifying the following as teaching strategies that make an instructional difference:

- *Make overt connections* between and across the curriculum, students' lives, literature, and literacy.
- *Plan lessons that connect* with each other, with test demands, and with students' growing knowledge and skills.
- *Develop goals and strategies* that meet students' needs and are intrinsically connected to the larger curriculum.
- *Weave even unexpected intrusions* into integrated experiences for students.

Making connections helps sustain the instructional narrative of our curriculum, for without these connections, lessons become discrete items that have no apparent meaning or relationship to each other besides their existence on the test at the end of the unit. Thus not only should the students be making connections, but we, too, so that our curriculum adds up to a conversation worth having, a story worth telling, a class worth attending.

8 *Develop and use skills and knowledge in the context of meaningful conversations.*

Conversations come in various forms; we can have them with ourselves, classmates, or those in the public arena. We can have such conversations in writing (e.g., journals, response logs, blogs) or through actual spoken discussions (e.g., class and group discussions, literature circles). By "conversation" I mean to emphasize the content, not the means, for written conversations with the self are just as meaningful as spoken conversations with others in a group. Applebee (1996) said in his *Curriculum as Conversation:*

> The notion that learners are to construct their own understandings leads in turn to new ways of thinking about the role of the teacher, and has generated such now-familiar terms as scaffolding, reciprocal teaching, apprenticeship, and mentoring. From our present perspective, this previous work on instruction provides new and more powerful ways of thinking about how students can best be helped to enter into important domains for conversation. Only in conversation guided by others will students develop the tacit knowledge necessary to participate on their own.

In subsequent studies of the role of conversation, Applebee and Langer (Partnership for Literacy paper, 2006) found that "Other aspects of cognitively engaging instruction, however, had a longer trajectory of continual development across two years of participation. The ability to sustain open discussion, to ask authentic questions, to ask higher order questions, to support envisionment building, and to foster extended curricular conversations all saw some growth during the first year and continued growth during the second year." Further inquiries into adolescent literacy, particularly as related to closing the achievement gap, confirm the notion that effective instruction is "dialogic" (CELA, 2003) since classroom talks are "an extended discussion in which comments build upon one another." In such classrooms:

- Students and teacher share and debate interpretations of texts.
- The teacher poses or gets the students to pose authentic questions.
- The teacher introduces strategies for generating understanding.
- The teacher provides support for all students to participate in reading, writing, and discussion.

What lingers long after the last bell has rung are the conversations that have led students to important discoveries about themselves, the world, and the texts they have read.

In both my AP and ACCESS classes, skills and knowledge are fundamental to the enterprise, but they are not what kids leave remembering. What lingers long after the last bell has rung are the conversations that have led students to important discoveries about themselves, the world, and the texts they have read. This push for meaningful, sustained conversations about and *through* different texts, both literary and informational, is the result of some of the most important research done in recent years (Copeland, 2005; Daniels, 2002; Langer and Close, 2001; Nystrand, 2006).

I use such conversations to solve a range of problems in my classroom. Large classes allow kids to disappear into the corners, avoiding potentially important encounters with texts and their peers; yet it is precisely these encounters with others that bring a class to life and help students see other perspectives. Thus literature circles or Socratic seminars not only transform one large-class discussion into many small-group discussions but also increase the level of engagement and accountability in the class by providing public performances for which the students must take responsibility.

The *50 Essential Lessons* emphasizes not only how to prepare kids to participate but how to teach them the skills needed to make meaningful contributions to discussions. Through use of the tools and the techniques that I demonstrate, students can develop the academic sensibility they need to determine what information or ideas are worth sharing and how to respond to the ideas of others. This is particularly important with students who lack an understanding of what to actually talk about when discussing a text. Too often, low-performing students get only a heavy, steady dose of skills instruction and are never given the chance to enter into the "great conversation" by voicing their ideas. Thus teachers who wish to engage all students will ensure the following (CELA newsletter, 2003):

- All students are expected to have interesting and relevant ideas, questions, hunches, and understandings.
- Multiple perspectives are treated as ways to enrich understandings.
- Students explain and defend their points of view using supporting evidence in texts and their own experiences.
- [They] support envisionment building by ensuring students develop effective strategies for developing understanding and for participating.

Each of the fifty lessons models the kind of classroom environment encouraged by the list above and provides the opportunity for an extended conversation with your students.

Each of the ten guiding principles I am outlining in this teacher's guide complement the others in various ways. Central to this particular principle is the call not only to have meaningful conversations but to teach students, especially those from backgrounds who lack them, the skills and knowledge to enter into and contribute to these discussions. An additional way of doing this is to provide these students with the language, such as academic vocabulary (Burke, 2004; Marzano, 2004), needed to participate in academic discourse; another, which we will examine in the next section, is to show them what these skills look like in the context of the class by modeling a successful performance.

 Know what a successful performance looks like on all tasks and assessments.

If you want to watch a successful learning process, watch boys playing a video game. They observe what others do to master the moves, the controls, and the features (Gee, 2004; Johnson, 2005; Smith and Wilhelm, 2002). They study others' performances to learn how to complete the task themselves, moving through the novice stage and along the continuum toward mastery within a relatively short period of time due to the feedback they get from the game and their friends (who are yelling advice all around them in a very social, interactive learning environment). The moves that lead to success are, in short, demonstrated but also demystified (Levine, 2003): the players see that there are concrete steps they can take to achieve the desired outcome and thus feel capable and supported.

If you want to watch a successful learning process, watch boys playing a video game.

Classes are not always like that; in fact, they often seem to be places where, as George Hillocks often reminds us, kids show up expected to do what they have not yet been taught. Students frequently feel about as oriented and prepared to succeed as most of us would if we sat down on a couch, picked up the controller, and played *Halo* or some other complex computer game, expecting to win the first time we played it.

Throughout the lessons, you will find me standing at the overhead modeling what I want students to do. I am a bit like the coach who stands at the board drawing diagrams of who will do what on a given play in the upcoming game: a coach wants the players to see what they must do, to develop a visual schema of what the well-done job will look like so players can evaluate their performance against the standard. A coach might even show a video from a game, following that up with a demonstration on the field. This teacher-modeling is a fundamental part of every student's cognitive development (Vygotsky, 1978), particularly if the student comes from a background in which academic tasks seem foreign (Delpit, 1996). Thus students at all levels need to see what it looks like to write a certain way, use a particular tool, or discuss a text in a specific way. If I am introducing a new technique, such as collaborative reading, I will pull up a chair and huddle up with a student so I can demonstrate the technique to the full class or to a group that needs some extra guidance, whether it is in an AP or ACCESS class. If I am using a new tool, I will put a blank one on the overhead and show students how to use it, thinking aloud as I do so, before asking them to try it. Afterward, I will check their level of proficiency before I turn them loose to try it again on their own.

Another key element to this principle is teaching students to understand the criteria by which they will be assessed. Some of the lessons show students examining the scoring guidelines from the College Board or state exit exam, using those criteria to evaluate sample papers before writing their own and using the same rubric to evaluate their work. I put those samples on the overhead and in their hands so they can study these performances, determining for themselves or through group discussions what makes them effective or flawed. In other circumstances, I will create samples myself, putting them on the overhead and, when appropriate, using color or other textual features to help students see the different elements of a performance, demystifying the process for them by showing how I achieved success, and then thinking aloud about what I did as well as how and why I did it before letting them do the same task on their own. I will also bring in student samples from current or past classes, which we then analyze, using these models to drive the cycle of improvement instead of treating each assignment as a conclusion, an end point.

One of the most effective ways to obtain examples and have them readily available is to copy student exemplars when work is turned in and to keep these exemplars with your lesson plans. In my Master Binder (Burke, 2003), I keep each day's lesson plan, along with copies of any handouts, transparencies, and samples I will use; once student work comes in, whether a paper or a completed tool, I copy representative examples for the next year, attaching them in the Master Binder to the original assignment. I then use these examples to raise the bar and encourage even better performances from subsequent classes. Students in my AP class, for example, had to perform *Rosencrantz & Guildenstern Are Dead* (Stoppard) as part of their final. I showed them excerpts from the film adaptation to give them a sense of the play; more importantly, however, I retained a copy of one group's brilliant DVD of a scene. I will show that scene to my students next year, telling them this is the minimum standard and that it represents what I expect. By providing students with a model in the coming year, thanks to this wonderful DVD scene my previous students created, my new students will see the standard, as well as the criteria by which their performance will be evaluated.

Everyone needs a goal, an objective; a *standard* is, in its original meaning, a flag raised to create a rallying point (Jago, 2001) toward which all should aspire; it is an "invitation to struggle," as is said of the Constitution and its lofty ideals.

 ## Read a variety of types of texts, including multimedia and visual.

Previously, in principle #5, I discussed *communicating* by multiple means and other media; this final principle, in contrast, emphasizes the other side of "textual intelligence": *reading* a wide range of texts, which students must ultimately be able to analyze, write about, and discuss by the means outlined under principle #5. All major reports on literacy (Alliance for Excellent Education, 2004; Conley, 2005; Intersegmental Committee, 2002; National Council of Teachers of English, 2006; Partnership for 21st Century Skills, 2005) stress the "21st century" literacies, which focus increasingly on a range of not only *types* of texts but the means and media we must master if we are to effectively read those texts, which are no longer fixed in time and on paper by the permanence of ink. One need only look at a current social studies textbook, with all its text types—words, images, infographics, Web sites, and visuals such as maps—to realize that book pages have become, in form and function, more like Web pages in their use of colors, links, and content. They call for a different way of reading, a modern literacy that I have explored in my recent books *Illuminating Texts* (2000), *Reading Reminders* (2001), *The Reader's Handbook* (2003), and *ACCESSing Schools* (2005). NCTE sums up adolescent literacy in its policy research brief (2006) in the following "broad range of domains" students will encounter in the world for which we are preparing them:

- Analyzing arguments
- Comparing editorial viewpoints
- Decoding nutrition information on food packaging
- Assembling furniture
- Taking doses of medicine correctly
- Determining whether to vote for a state amendment
- Interpreting medical tables
- Identifying locations on a map
- Finding information online

To these adult literacies, we must add such academic literacies as reading or critically viewing videos, Web sites, textbooks, articles, literary texts, and tests of many different types.

The guiding principles outlined above, and the *50 Essential Lessons* that grew out of these principles, offer teachers a way to "apprentice" (Schoenbach, Greenleaf, Cziko, and Hurwitz, 1999) their students by providing students with the tools and techniques they need to make meaning from multiple types of texts, ultimately enabling students to go out and make a living in a complex world. Hopefully, the "essential" lessons they learn here will guide and carry them into the future—a future that is not just theirs, but *ours*.

🔘 **Tools** can be found on the accompanying CD–ROM.

Texts marked with an asterisk (*) can be found in *Tools & Texts*. Other listed text titles are those used in Jim's model lessons and can typically be found in English classroom resource collections.

> " One day while I sat in Starbucks having coffee, I noticed two young women in Starbucks aprons, each of whom had two three-inch-thick binders, complete with laser-printed tabs and indexes. When I asked them if they had to read all *that* just to make me a latté and serve me a scone, they both rolled their eyes and said yes.
>
> Our society and the workplace demand more reading than ever. Kids need specific reading skills if they are to move through the world with the confidence and skill we know they need."

–The English Teacher's Companion, p. 28–29

Reading

LESSONS **1 – 15**

NOTES

continued on following page

● **Tools** can be found on the accompanying CD–ROM.

Texts marked with an asterisk (*) can be found in *Tools & Texts*. Other listed text titles are those used in Jim's model lessons and can typically be found in English classroom resource collections.

NOTES

Make Connections

Effective readers make connections to the text to help them understand, remember, and enjoy what they read.

Essential Skill Set

▶ **Make** connections to yourself, other texts, and the world.

▶ **Identify** common subjects on which to base connections.

▶ **Generate** questions needed to make connections.

▶ **Use** these connections to improve comprehension and help you write.

Frame the Lesson

STUDENTS AT ALL LEVELS STRUGGLE AT ONE TIME OR ANOTHER TO UNDERSTAND, REMEMBER, or enjoy what they read. Many subjects and texts that kids read become mere lists of facts to know for a test, an ironic outcome given that when teachers read they constantly make connections to themselves, to events that happened earlier in the text, to other texts they have read by this author or about this subject, and to ideas in the text that connect to the world at large. This lesson teaches students how to make connections with the texts they read.

Gather and Prepare

The model lesson uses students' Sustained Silent Reading books. You can use the sequence for a class novel or short story if you prefer. Once students are familiar with the Making the Connection tool, they can use it with many types of texts.

▶ Make copies of the **Making the Connection** tool for each student.

▶ After reading the model lesson, reflect on your personal reading. Choose a book with connections you can share. Jot down ideas on a Making the Connection tool to show as a model.

▶ Make notes for adapting the model lesson to your class.

Jamil and Joe turn to discuss their personal connections after reading. They do this to get ideas and to see how others complete the task.

Get kids thinking about making connections.

Teach

ANYONE EVER BEEN STRANDED ON AN ISLAND with no hope of getting off?

CLASS: What? Of course not!

How about growing up in the South in a small town back in the 1940s? Or going to war? Anyone do that? How about living in Egypt—thousands of years ago?

CLASS: What are you talking about, Mr. Burke?

These are the kinds of things your teachers ask you to read about all the time, right? You read *To Kill a Mockingbird*, but it's set in a different time and place—the world was very different then. Or you read *Lord of the Flies* about a bunch of boys stranded on a remote island with no adults—except you've never been on an island, or you're not a boy, or you don't know much about England. What do you do? What can help you understand and remember and write about these things you read about in novels and also in textbooks for your other subjects? Anyone have something specific you do?

ARIANNA: Sometimes I ask myself if I've been in a situation like that and what it was like. That helps me see it better and imagine what is going on. Like when we read *Lord of the Flies*. A lot of it reminded me of summer camp–for example, the way kids would go around in groups and gang up on someone in the cabin…treat them like the boys did Piggy.

That's great, Arianna. I like the way you explained that, also.

Why should we do this…make these connections?

ALEXANDRA: It makes the story more interesting because you can relate to it more.

Generate reasons for making connections.

Definitely true. You may not know what it was like back in the time of Shakespeare, but you know what Romeo and Juliet are all about. So if you think about what you or your friends go through, it makes it much more personal. What else?

EVAN: If you connect things, it is so much easier to remember them. The ideas become like lights on a Christmas tree–all connected. When you think of one, others light up and make it easier to remember.

Wow, that's a great analogy, Evan. I like that.

 The **Making the Connection** tool can be found on the CD-ROM.

So far we have: connections help you understand it and remember it better.

We extend the conversation for a bit to generate a few more reasons. I begin showing them, through examples, how they can use this skill to improve their performance in this and other classes.

I'll give you a quick example of how I make connections when I read. Recently, I read *The South Beach Diet* and even though it was about losing weight and eating better, I kept relating it to teaching. I know that sounds crazy, but it made it much more interesting to me and helped me understand not just dieting but teaching and learning in some new ways.

I put a transparency of the Making the Connection handout on the overhead while kids pass out the same sheet to the class.

Let's try making connections using the books you are each reading for silent reading. Before you begin, let's look at a tool to help you do this. The Making the Connection tool reminds you that there are three types of connections—Personal, Text, and Other Text or World—you can make. Because this is new to some of you, for now we will just focus on personal connections. After all, isn't it all about *us?* Cross out the other boxes, and as you read, jot down words that come to mind. We will only focus on one area for now to make it easier to learn how to do this.

Here's an example I did last night so you could see what it looks like when you are finished. I was reading *A Perfect Peace* by Amos Oz. In the book one character thinks about leaving Israel to live in America. Another character starts criticizing America. So one of my personal connection words was "America." Moving down the tool here, I entered "America" in the Subject box and came up with three questions to help me explore my personal connections about this subject: 1. "What do I like about America?" 2. "What don't I like about America?" 3. "Did living in Africa (which I did for two years with the Peace Corps) affect how I felt about America?"

For now, we aren't going to do the other parts of the tool; I just want you to learn to make personal connections first. We can work on the other stuff later. So go ahead and read and jot down words in the Personal Connection box while reading and after you finish.

Now that you've got some words, go through and choose *one* from the list and put it in the Subject box. That will be the subject of your writing. Then take a moment and jot down a few questions that would help you write about that. Keep in mind the example I gave you about my book a bit ago.

They write down their questions.

Okay. Now we're all set, ready to make a claim about the subject. Look in the Main Idea box. Here's my example about my own subject of America. In the Main Idea box, I have written, "I feel about America the way some kids feel about their fathers." This is a personal connection because I am drawing on my own feelings and experiences to comment about the subject. Then I will go ahead and write my paragraph, using that line as my focus line. Go ahead and write your own main idea about your subject.

After they have done this, we discuss some of their main idea statements before they write. This allows us to talk about the importance of the clarity of their statement in relation to the clarity of their writing.

Model making a personal connection.

Help kids find a subject, generate questions, and form a main idea.

Jongyup, Michael, and Joe compare their main idea statements in order to refine them before they write their paragraphs.

Assess and Extend

If students are learning
how to make personal
connections…

▶ **ASSESS STUDENTS' PERSONAL CONNECTIONS** Collect the
Making the Connection tools and assess how students did.
Copy examples to an overhead transparency so you can discuss
them the next day. In the discussion, generate guidelines to help
students determine if something is a personal connection. For
example: It has *I*, *me*, or *we* in it, Andrew says.

If students are ready to make
other types of connections…

▶ **MAKE TEXT AND OTHER TEXT/WORLD CONNECTIONS**
Repeat this lesson (or some variation on it), focusing
only on personal connections till students reach
mastery. Then move on to make text
connections and eventually other text/world
connections. Provide new copies of the Making
the Connection tool for each type of connection
until students can follow the directions independently.

If students are ready
to write…

▶ **USE THE TOOL TO WRITE ABOUT CONNECTIONS** When students show that
they "get it," use the completed tool to work on writing skills while reinforcing what they
have learned about making different types of connections. The directions on the tool
explain this process.

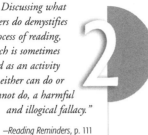

Discussing what readers do demystifies the process of reading, which is sometimes perceived as an activity people either can do or cannot do, a harmful and illogical fallacy.

—*Reading Reminders*, p. 111

Use a Reading Process

Effective readers use a reading process to understand and remember important details from a variety of types of text.

Essential Skill Set

▶ **Identify** what you do when you read.

▶ **Analyze** how, when, and why you do these things while reading.

▶ **Synthesize** and apply strategies in the reading process.

After reading an assigned text, Anthony analyzes what he does when he reads, including how and when he does it, to better understand his reading process.

Frame the Lesson

ALL STUDENTS FACE CHALLENGES WHEN READING—OR THEY SHOULD. If they are not striving to make meaning, they are reading texts that do not challenge them to reach beyond their established abilities. Students at all levels benefit from analyzing their reading "game," just as athletes do when they study their own and others' moves. While some students may resist this lesson at first, thinking it is somehow "remedial," they inevitably find it interesting and useful because it helps them to understand how they read and what they can do to revise their process when it breaks down. Students can analyze their reading process with any text that challenges them within reason.

Gather and Prepare

I begin this lesson by making connections between the reading process and other processes students use in their lives; you can adapt the discussion for your students. Then my students read W. B. Yeats' poem "The Second Coming" and monitor their reading process. You can use this poem, which is in *Texts and Tools*, or select a text that is appropriate for your class. The lesson can be adapted for different types of texts.

▶ Make copies of the **Episodic Notes** tool and the **Reading Process Self-Evaluation** for each student.

▶ After reading the model lesson, decide whether to use "The Second Coming" or choose another text. Preview it and jot down notes about your reading process. This will help you anticipate your students' needs and responses.

▶ Decide whether to introduce the text or let students begin reading on their own. (See "Assess and Extend.")

▶ Fill in an Episodic Notes tool to show students a visual representation of your reading process.

▶ Complete a Reading Process Self-Evaluation to familiarize yourself with this tool.

Teach

LAST WEEKEND I WAS WATCHING MY SON AT AN INDOOR ROCK-CLIMBING PLACE. It had all these walls that look like the sides of mountains with colored tape that showed climbers the path they should follow to reach the top. What was interesting to me was how the climbers would talk about what they just did when they made their climb.

When I asked one of them why he did that, he said that if you didn't talk about it, it was hard to figure out what you did and you might not be able to repeat it. This reminded me of what good readers do when they read. Reading a difficult poem, for example, is a lot like making a difficult climb up the side of a mountain: you have to use different techniques to overcome all the obstacles and complete your climb.

I know this seems like a rather strange analogy when discussing reading, but lately people have been struggling to understand what we have read, so I thought we should take a day to back up and look at the process you use to understand what you read.

Joe, what does the football team do first thing Monday after a weekend game?

JOE: We watch the game tapes to see what we did. Coach yells at us, tells us what we did right and wrong. It really helps you see things.

That's right. To better understand why you won or lost—so you can repeat that performance if it was good or improve upon it the next time, right? Reading is the same way: you have to know what you do to understand something so you can try other strategies when you don't. And just like in football, where you don't run the same play against every team every time, different texts need to be read different ways depending on why you are reading them.

Before we start looking at reading, let's think about things you had to learn to be good at. Make a list of things—it doesn't matter what they are so long as you had to learn to be good at them. It could be video games, skateboarding, dancing, singing, designing Web pages, or creating art—I don't care, so long as you had to learn and work to do it well. Pick one of the items from your list and quickly jot down what you do that allows you to be successful. How, for example, do you learn and become good at a new video game or dance step? Break it down into the steps you follow. What do you do first? Why? What do you do during the process of learning? How about after—what do you do after you finish playing the game for the first time or complete the routine?

I give them time to do this; then I have them share what they did for a few minutes so they can all get a chance to shine, to feel good about something they do well. Then we discuss briefly how they got good at these things, and I jot down on the board responses such as "trial and error" and "watched others do it."

Now let's try reading. I'm going to give you a text that will challenge you but that I think you can understand on some level: W. B. Yeat's "The Second Coming." I know there is stuff in this poem you will not understand. Don't worry about that. It's supposed to be hard so you can show us both—yourself and me—how you figure something out when you don't understand it.

As I talk, I hand out the Episodic Notes tool and the poem. The poem has to be difficult to force students to use various strategies to try to "climb" the text. If the text is too easy, they will just "get it" and defeat the purpose, which is to make them aware of the process they employ in order to understand what they read.

Read the poem and pay attention to what you do as you read. Use the Episodic Notes tool to organize your response; use the three boxes to draw what you do before, during, and after you read the text. You *must* represent your process visually by showing what happens at each step: before, during, and after you read. Your drawings can look like a comic strip, a flow chart—anything that illustrates your reading process. Then, when you finish, use the lined areas next to the boxes to explain what your drawings show.

When you are finished, compare your strategies to see what other students did when they read. Also, look at how they did the assignment. If someone else used the tool a different way, acknowledge that there are always other ways to solve a problem, some more effective and others less effective than your way.

After they have talked for a few minutes, we debrief and I write some of the strategies they discovered on the board, for example, "make pictures in my head," "ask questions," "translate it into my own wording if I don't understand it."

Now I want to push you to be a bit more analytical about your process by asking you to analyze *how* and *why* you do these different things when reading. So, for example, if you say that you "make movies in your head" or "visualize" when you read, I want to know how you do that and why. To help you be more organized about this, divide a sheet of paper into three columns and label them with these headers: What I Do, How I Do It, and Why I Do It. Let me give you an example so you'll know what a charting strategy looks like. I'll do it on the board so you can all see.

What I Do
- Make a movie in my head

How I Do It
- Ask questions like "What does it look like?"
- Connect what I am reading to places I have been or seen to help me see it better

Why I Do It
- Helps me understand and enjoy it because I can see and hear what it is saying

Give kids time to fill in their charts before contributing to the class chart.

Let's talk about what you do. I'll just add your details to my "What" list on the board so we can make a good list of what you do that helps you understand what you read. *(A discussion follows.)*

Here's a handout called the Reading Process Self-Evaluation, which gives you another way to think about what we have done today. Go through and circle the words that best describe what you do in each stage of the reading process. When you finish, turn the page over and write a reflection about what you noticed about your reading process based on our work today.

Have students use the Episodic Notes tool to visualize their reading process.

A student visualizes a scene from *Hamlet* to improve her understanding of the text, a strategy many of my students use in their reading process.

Analyze the reading process by charting strategies.

Have students do a Reading Process Self-Evaluation.

The **Reading Process Self-Evaluation** tool can be found on the CD-ROM.

Assess and Extend

If students are ready to write about the reading process…

▶ **WRITE A PROCESS ANALYSIS ESSAY** After this sequence, have students use their notes and their Reading Process Self-Evaluation as the basis for a process analysis essay in which they reflect on and explain their reading process, using examples from your class today and their other classes.

If students need more help…

▶ **ASK SCAFFOLDING QUESTIONS** For students who are just learning to use a reading process, or who have trouble understanding the text, provide more support. *Before they read,* make explicit what they must do before, during, and after. You can do this collaboratively by asking, for example, "What question should you try to answer when reading this text?" *While they read,* interrupt them when it seems appropriate and ask them to reflect on what they are struggling to understand and how they tried to solve that problem. "What worked—and why—to help you understand?" *When they finish,* have them reflect on what strategies they used that were particularly effective or ineffective and why. Take time to discuss or write about this, asking kids to go into some detail about how they used a particular strategy and how it helped them. If possible, extend this discussion to include their experience reading other texts in different subject areas such as science and history.

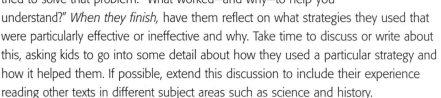

*"Readers must also
learn to adjust their purpose
when reading, knowing
how to focus on one aspect
of a text that might, for
example, shape its meaning
more than others."*

—Reading Reminders, p. 162

3 Develop a Purpose Question

*Effective readers establish a purpose before
they begin reading to improve comprehension
and help evaluate the importance of information.*

Essential Skill Set

▶ **Determine** why you are
reading a particular text.

▶ **Preview** the text,
paying close attention
to the title, headers,
and captions.

▶ **Develop** a Purpose
Question (PQ)
appropriate to the
task and text.

▶ **Evaluate** the details of
what you read in light of
your purpose question.

Frame the Lesson

WHILE IT IS USEFUL TO HAVE A PURPOSE IN MIND WHEN READING FICTION, it is essential when
reading expository writing since we are likely to be reading it to learn something or find
information related to a larger task such as a research paper or document-based essay.
Students tend to be reckless readers and so will often throw themselves into a text without
determining why they are reading it. This lesson shows them how to develop a purpose
question and why they should.

Gather and Prepare

In the model lesson, my students read "Robo-
Legs," an article provided in *Tools and Texts*.
The Article Notes tool and the sequence in this
lesson can be used with any expository article
that fits your students' needs or interests.
Current issues of magazines and newspapers
are sources of timely, relevant articles.

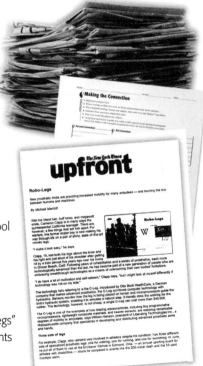

▶ After reading this lesson, evaluate the text your
students will read. Generate several possible
purpose questions. Fill out an Article Notes tool
to see how it works with the text.

▶ Make copies of the **Article Notes**
tool for each student. Also make an
overhead transparency.

▶ Make copies of "Robo-Legs"
or the article your students
will read.

Shannel skims an article to gather some initial details,
which she will then use to answer her purpose question
and complete her Article Notes.

● The **"Robo-Legs" article** and the **Article Notes** tool can
be found on the CD-ROM.

Teach

YOGI BERRA USED TO SAY SOMETHING LIKE "If you don't know where you're going, how will you know when you get there?" Well, reading is kind of like that; you can't just belly flop into an article or a chapter in a textbook. You read stuff like that to learn something specific, to find out how one thing led to another, or how one group is different from another. You have to have a destination in mind. When you go to the airport, you don't just grab *any* plane. You look for the gate that will get you to your final point. This allows you to evaluate the importance of every sign, all the monitors in the airport, the information on your plane ticket, and the signs at each gate, as they relate to your purpose, which is to find the right plane going to the right place.

When I read something for information, such as an article, I am doing so for a purpose. Maybe I am reading it to find out about a particular teaching method or to determine if some plant will thrive in my backyard. So here is a really cool article about "robo legs" and a copy of the Article Notes tool, which I created to help us read for a purpose.

I pass out the article and the Article Notes tool and put a copy of the tool on the overhead for reference.

Before we get started, take a second to fill in the title, author, and subject (based on a quick glance at the title and subtitle). It's important to keep track of such information when reading for a purpose. Often, when reading such articles for a paper, you need to cite them and so you need some minimal information about where the information came from.

Okay, so take a look at the title and subtitle and think about what kind of PQ we could generate for this article. The title is "Robo-Legs" and the subtitle is "New prosthetic limbs are providing increased mobility for many amputees—and blurring the line between humans and machines." So what is a good question to be able to answer by the time you finish reading this article?

JOE: "What are Robo-Legs?"

The **Article Notes** tool can be found on the CD-ROM.

That's a great start and a good question on its own. Before we write anything down, let's ask if there are others we should consider.

MONICA: "What does 'prosthetic' mean?"

That is a great word to put in the Vocabulary box there on the side of the page, but it's a bit too specific. Important, though. What other questions might we ask?

MICHAEL: "How are the new prosthetic legs different from the old ones?"

That's another great question. But what about that part about "blurring the lines between humans and machines"? That seems an interesting but also important part of the article.

ALEX: How 'bout "How are the lines between humans and machines getting blurred?"

All right. Now let's see if we can combine these ideas into a PQ.

On my overhead transparency of the Article Notes, I write, "What are 'robo-legs'—and how are they 'blurring the line between humans and machines'?" Everyone agrees this is good, and so I tell them to write it down on their sheets.

Now we know what we are setting out to learn, so let's move on.

Before we read the whole article, I want to show you how much information you can gather from an article in just a few minutes. This also helps you get a sense of the text, how hard it will be, how long it might take. Mostly though it gives you sort of a rough-draft understanding. So skim through the article by doing this: read the title, subtitle, headers, first and last paragraphs, and the first sentence of each paragraph. Do this in three minutes and then jot down three things you learned in the Preview section of the Article Notes.

Three minutes pass while they skim.

It doesn't matter if you are finished skimming. Just write down three things you learned. *(As they call them out, I add them to my sample on the overhead.)* Now think about this tonight at home when you have to read a chapter on eating disorders in Health or the creation of the United Nations in History: in just *three minutes*, you have a lot of information, not all of it, but a good beginning, which helps you read better, remember it better, and answer your PQ.

Now you're ready. Read the article, and as you read, underline any details that are related to your PQ. In other words, if you see some information that will help you answer the PQ, underline the key words—not all of it. Then when you finish, fill in the Pause and Reflect section of the Article Notes and, using those notes, *answer* the PQ and explain the author's main idea about it in Step 4.

After they finish,…

Since we all had the same PQ, our notes should match up pretty well. Turn to a neighbor and compare your notes with theirs. Don't just focus on what they wrote down: pay attention to how they took their notes. If they have something different than you, ask them why they wrote that down and how they came up with it. If you realize something you did not before, feel free to revise your notes in light of your new understanding.

After they discuss for a bit,…

Okay, everyone has had time to compare and discuss. Let's take the last few minutes to see what you came up with. Since our focus is on developing a PQ, let's start with that. Are there other PQs you could develop for this article?

Yes, Monica—what else could we ask?

> **MONICA:** You could ask something like, "How are these legs made?"

That's good. Any others——questions this article answers but that are different than the one we asked as our PQ?

> **MICHAEL:** "We could ask something about how they feel about losing their limbs, or something."

That's a good question, Michael. They all are. The point is that there are usually many reasons you can read a text. Sometimes someone, like your teacher, or a test gives you a reason; on other occasions, you must develop one on your own, but either way the PQ should help you complete the task at hand.

Preview the text in three minutes.

Read, evaluate details, and answer the PQ using Article Notes.

Have students compare Article Notes.

Identify other PQs appropriate to the text.

Students compare their information, discussing and analyzing any differences.

Assess and Extend

If students need to work on test preparation skills…

▶ **ANSWER QUESTIONS ON THE ARTICLE NOTES** To integrate test preparation skills, have students complete Step 5 on the Article Notes, the Factual and Inferential questions, and then answer them on the back. Discuss why these are such important questions.

If students need to work on academic discussion…

▶ **USE THE BONUS TO EXPAND DISCUSSION** To provide the opportunity for students to participate in an academic discussion, have them do the Bonus by going up to the board and writing down questions or comments they have and want to talk about in class. This mimics a chat room online, where everyone is free to speak up; it also makes the class more active, giving the students a chance to determine what the class will talk about. You can then draw from the board and use those questions to facilitate the discussion about the article and their PQ, which, by this time, they have answered and are now exploring in greater depth.

As a bonus activity, if students need to work on academic discussion skills, have them write questions or comments they want to discuss in class. This mimics an online chat room, where everyone is free to speak up. Here's an example of my students' questions to another article.

" *Evaluating importance is an essential ability to master quickly so they can apply it to their reading in other classes; without it they are unable to prepare for tests, take notes, or take tests because all information seems equally important—or, to some, unimportant.*"

—ACCESSing School, p. 91

4

Identify Main Ideas and Supporting Details

Effective readers identify the main ideas and their supporting details.

Essential Skill Set

▶ **Preview** to determine the subject of the text.

▶ **Identify** the main idea and supporting details of each paragraph.

▶ **Determine** which details help to support or illustrate the main ideas of the text.

Andrew uses his highlighter to identify the main ideas as he reads the article; he uses the other pen to label the supporting details.

Frame the Lesson

INFORMATIONAL TEXTS MAKE UP THE BULK OF STUDENTS' READING in school and the workplace. Textbooks represent the largest share of such reading in the middle and high school years, though supplemental articles run a close second. Such texts are organized around the main ideas of each larger subject; carefully arranged within those main ideas are the examples, details, and commentary that make up the "supporting details." Being able to figure out the main idea and its supporting details is essential to several core academic skills: reading, taking notes, and taking tests.

Gather and Prepare

In the model lesson, my students identify main ideas and details in an article about the digestive system called "Burp, Rumble, Toot! How your lunch can turn you into a one-person band." The article is provided in *Tools and Texts*; however, you can use any informational text for this lesson. Newspapers and current issues of magazines about science or history are sources for timely, relevant articles. A textbook excerpt also works if you can copy it for students to highlight.

▶ After reading the model lesson, evaluate the article your students will read. Note points you want to preview or discuss with your students.

▶ Prepare an overhead transparency of the text.

▶ Make copies of the article for each student.

▶ Provide extra highlighters or colored pencils.

▶ Make copies of the **Main Idea Organizer** for each student if you plan to extend the lesson to writing. (See "Assess and Extend".)

Teach

MANY OF YOU HAVE STRUGGLED IN DIFFERENT CLASSES when reading articles and textbooks about different subjects. I know History has given people trouble; many had a hard time in Health. You have to read informational articles about subjects that are often new to you. You have to take notes on what you read. And then, as if that weren't enough, you usually have to take a test on it all!

I want to use our time today to look at a great article, one I think you'll all find interesting, that also gives us a chance to learn how to do something better: identify the main ideas in what you read and the details related to that main idea. This skill is essential when reading anything, but it's especially important for expository writing like essays, articles, and textbooks. I chose this article today because I know many of you are struggling in Health and this is an article about the digestive system and how it works. It's called "Burp, Rumble, Toot! How your lunch can turn you into a one-person band."

Everyone needs to come up and get a copy of the article and two crayons or highlighters—two *different* colors.

Highlighters are best but expensive. I have a mishmash of colored pencils, highlighters, and crayons kids can use if they do not have their own. In a pinch, kids can use different underlining patterns, for example, solid line, dotted line, or squiggly line, instead of colors.

One of the things you have to do when you are reading an informational piece of writing is get the big picture. What do I mean by the "big picture"? Can anyone tell me?

LUIS: Like, you know what the whole thing is about.

How can you figure that out, though, without reading it?

ALEXANDRA: You look at the title.

Let's do this…preview the article by doing what we have done before. Read the title, the subtitle, the opening and last paragraphs, and all the headings and captions. Then as soon as you are done, jot down three key things you learned from this article. Write them on the back or in your notebook.

We all read it together silently. I do this with them to model and to refresh myself for when we discuss it. When I am finished, I turn to the whiteboard and write the heading "Preview Notes" and under that a bullet point.

Okay, so you seem pretty much finished. What did you learn from the two-minute skim?

JOE: It's natural to make noises.

BRIANNA: We actually eat air.

JAMIL: We…ugh…pass gas *fourteen* times a day.

KENDRA: *(Wrinkling her nose.)* It's disgusting.

All right, good enough. Here is what I want you to do. Each paragraph has a main idea. Some of them are harder to see than others. Those are called *implied* main ideas. We'll talk more about those when we find them. You need the article and the highlighters to do this.

Someone read aloud the first couple paragraphs, up to the heading that says "Eating Air." *(Someone volunteers and reads aloud.)*

Is there a main idea, like a topic sentence, in there anywhere?

MICHAEL: There is not really one sentence. It just sort of talks about all sorts of things the body does when it eats.

Good. So we could say it has an "implied" main idea. What does that mean, *implied? (When no one responds, I ask the question a different way....)* What does it mean when someone says, "What were you *implying* when you said that?"

BRANDON: It's like when someone says something but doesn't actually say it. They mean something extra…. It's hard to explain. What I mean is, they don't just come out and say what they mean.

Right. And that can make it hard to understand what someone is saying—or writing, right? We have to write the main idea for this section, since it's implied and we can't highlight it. We'll use Michael's statement: "The body makes a lot of noises when it eats." With a pen or pencil, write that in the margin. *(I make notes on the whiteboard while the kids write on their copies of the article.)*

Now let's look at the next section. What does it tell us?

I read the next paragraph aloud and ask what that paragraph is doing. We conclude that it is giving an example, so we make a note that identifies it as an example. After this, we come to a paragraph with a stated main idea and details that we can highlight.

Now I want you to read the next paragraph. I want you to highlight the *main idea.* Then, as you read, I want you to use the *other* color to highlight the supporting details. Let's do a bit of this together. The first sentence reads, "Drinking bubbly drinks, talking, chewing gum, and eating too quickly can cause you to swallow a lot of air." Everyone use one of your highlighters, crayons—whatever you have—to highlight that. That is your main idea color. I'll use red here on the overhead as an example. *(I have a transparency of the page to help them see what I am doing.)*

Someone read the next sentence aloud. *(After someone does, I go on.)* Thanks for reading that. What is that sentence doing,…what is it going on about?

CLASS: It tells you more about what happens. It gets more specific about the sentence before it.

Oh, very good. So it is a supporting detail then. Use the other color highlighter. So I want to use blue here for mine. *(I underline that sentence on the transparency.)* Now everyone read the rest of the paragraph and decide what it is: a main idea or a supporting detail. Then highlight it as you see fit.

We discuss what they did so I can check their initial understanding of the text and the technique.

Good! Now I want you to read through the rest of the article, color-coding the main idea and supporting details in each paragraph. If you come to something you aren't sure about, call me over and I'll help you figure out how to handle it.

After you finish highlighting the article, I want you to get together with one or two others and compare what you did to what they did. If they highlighted something differently, work through your differences until you can agree whether it is a main idea or supporting detail. Remember: there really can only be one main idea in a paragraph.

When an opportunity arises, identify implied main ideas.

Show students how to highlight main ideas and supporting details.

Have students finish highlighting and then compare with a partner.

They work and I check on their progress and offer support as needed. A few minutes before the bell, I gather their attention to review.

Review the relationship between main ideas and supporting details.

We're just about out of time, but let's go over some ideas from what we studied today. Where are you likely to find the main idea?

MARCUS: Usually at the beginning of the paragraph, but sometimes they put it at the end, which makes all the ideas that came before it work as supporting details.

Well said! What about the supporting details? What is the relationship between those and the main idea? That is, what are they *doing*?

SEVERAL STUDENTS MAKE SUGGESTIONS: Sometimes they get more specific about it…give you examples…explain or comment on the ideas…

Make connections to FODP in writing.

Those are all good ideas. The same ones we talk about when we discuss our own writing. What do we say? Good writing has to have FODP. What is that again? Good writing has to have…

Focus…Organization…Development…Purpose, they chant almost in unison since I ask this all the time.

So main idea is like focus. You take the subject and what the paragraph says about the subject and you get the focus. As for details, those are like the development, right? So keep these things in mind when you do your Health or History homework tonight: take notes on those main ideas.

Assess and Extend

If students are ready to work on writing skills…

▶ **APPLY TO WRITING** Have students use a Main Idea Organizer to organize their notes for this article. Help them see the distinction between the main idea and the details as reflected by the organizer. Then have them use their organizer notes to write a paragraph with FODP. (The Main Idea Organizer is in *Tools and Texts*. Also, see Lesson 5.)

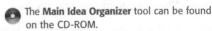

The **Main Idea Organizer** tool can be found on the CD-ROM.

If students need to work on finding main ideas and details in paragraphs…

▶ **FOCUS ON A PARAGRAPH** Repeat the sequence, though not with an entire article. Instead, bring in exemplary paragraphs or write them yourself, using color-coding on the computer to distinguish between the main idea and the supporting details.

If students need help identifying the main idea and details in a paragraph…

▶ **GIVE THEM A MODEL PARAGRAPH CUT INTO SENTENCE STRIPS** Have them work together and manipulate the strips and then analyze how they identified the main idea and supporting details.

"Educe means 'to draw out,' and so we do with each question, draw ourselves further out into the world of uncertainty and amazed understanding...."

—*The English Teacher's Companion*, p. 253

Draw Conclusions from What You Read

Effective readers draw conclusions about the meaning and purpose of what they read.

Essential Skill Set

▶ **Draw** conclusions about what a work of fiction or expository prose means.

▶ **Establish** a purpose that helps you evaluate the importance of information.

▶ **Identify** the most important details according to your purpose.

▶ **Draw** conclusions based on those details.

Frame the Lesson

IN ALL ACADEMIC SUBJECTS, STUDENTS READ TEXTS, BOTH LITERARY AND EXPOSITORY, about which they must draw conclusions regarding people, trends, events, or ideas. In this lesson, my students read an article and draw conclusions about a public speaking program they will be participating in. The teaching sequence in the lesson is easily adapted to other texts and situations. If your students are just beginning to learn about drawing conclusions, see "Assess and Extend" for an alternate approach.

Gather and Prepare

In the model lesson, my students read "Messages from the Heart," an article about the demands and benefits of participating in Toastmasters International's Youth Leadership Program. The article is included in *Tools and Texts* for your reference. The strategies and tools in this lesson can be used with any expository text.

▶ Make copies of the **Main Idea Organizer** for each student. Also make an overhead transparency.

▶ After reading the lesson, consider the text you plan to teach. Decide whether to direct your students toward certain conclusions. I want my students to draw conclusions about what the Toastmasters International youth program is all about and why it's worth doing.

Arianna takes notes on the Main Idea Organizer to help her draw conclusions about the Toastmasters International Youth Leadership Program. She will use the notes to write an organized response to the article.

● The **Main Idea Organizer** tool can be found on the CD-ROM.

Teach

Help kids make connections to the article and to "drawing conclusions".

BEFORE WE BEGIN PARTICIPATING IN THE Toastmasters International Youth Leadership Program, we need to learn what the program is all about so you know what you will have to do and how the program will benefit you. I brought in an article this morning about the program and thought we would use it to also learn how to draw conclusions from what we read.

Anyone know what I mean by "draw conclusions"? This is a different way to use the word *draw* than most of you are used to. What does the word *draw* mean in this context?

No one offers an idea, which confirms my hunch that it's necessary to define these words.

Anyone ever had to get a blood test?

Immediately a bunch of kids squirm and announce their horror of needles. A ripple of chatter runs around the room.

Define what it means to "draw conclusions" and give examples from students' experience.

It seems a random question to ask, I know. What could a blood test possibly have to do with drawing conclusions? Anyone know?

KENDALL: Don't they say "draw blood" when they take your blood?

They do, yes. Very good, Miss Dittman. But what are they doing when they *draw* blood? How does a syringe actually do that?

JUAN: Well, they stick it in your arm and pull it out. It pulls your blood into those glass tube things. I hate that, man.

So when you *draw* something (not a picture), you are sort of pulling it out. What about *conclusions?* What are those?

JOE: That's the last paragraph in your essay.

Well, yes and no. It depends on what you do in that last paragraph. What does a writer usually try to accomplish in that last paragraph in an essay or an article?

JOE: They try to summarize what they have been saying.

Use what they know to help them understand what they don't.

Good, so if we put those two ideas together—*draw* meaning to pull out and *conclusion* meaning to summarize your main ideas—we get the idea that when we, the readers, draw conclusions, we have to pull out important details from the article and use them to draw a conclusion about what the writer is saying about a particular subject. For example, if a writer includes many startling facts and pieces of information about changes in the global workplace, we might draw the conclusion that the future will be more competitive and we need to be prepared to meet those challenges.

Your History classes ask you to draw conclusions all the time. You might get information about changes in immigration patterns or racial injustices, and you have to gather ideas from that information and use it to draw conclusions about what effect those changes had or how those injustices led, for example, to the civil rights movement.

This article we are reading today is about Toastmasters International's Youth Leadership Program, a public speaking program we are going to work with in the coming months. I am passing out two sheets: the article and a Main Idea Organizer. We'll set them up in a minute to help you take notes.

While kids pass out the pages, I place a transparency of the Main Idea Organizer on the overhead and shine it onto the whiteboard. I do this because it gives me more space to write.

In the Subject area, go ahead and write "Toastmasters program." Then skim the article to get a sense of what it is about. Just read the first lines of each paragraph and the last paragraph, and jot down two to three key facts about the program in the Subject area.

I give them a few minutes to skim the article. Then I make sure they understand the basic facts about the subject—who, what, when, and where, for example—before we proceed.

You can leave that Main Idea area blank for now, but in the first Detail column write "What students do"; in the second column, write "Benefits." In the third, write "What I think." These are your purpose questions to take notes on while you read. In the third column, I want you to draw conclusions about what the program is all about and why it's worth doing.

As you read, take notes in the appropriate box. Use bullets to set your ideas off from each other. For example, I might write "• *increases self-confidence*" in the Benefits column if I read something like that.

After students finish reading, I want them to use their notes to write a paragraph in which they synthesize the conclusions they have drawn about the program.

Because we have been focusing on paragraph organization lately, I want you to write a good paragraph using your notes, one that has FODP. Remind me—what does FODP stand for again?

CLASS: Focus…Organization…Development…Purpose….

So the focus is what?

ALEJANDRO: Toastmasters.

Right. We go to the Subject line and find "Toastmaster's program." What can we write in the Main Idea area that shows what we conclude about the program?

FANNY: Toastmasters program teaches kids to do public speaking and gives them much confidence.

I like that. Let's see if we can adjust it a bit so it's not limited to just confidence. *(We talk about it back and forth a bit.)* Okay, so here is what I have from our discussion: "Toastmasters benefits students in many ways by teaching them to speak in public and provide leadership." That's good. I like that.

I write it in the Main Idea area.

Now use that main idea to write your paragraph. Remember to use the organization of the Main Idea Organizer to give your paragraph organization and development.

Using the Main Idea Organizer, establish purposes for reading to help students identify the important details and draw conclusions.

Model how to use the tool and technique so students know what the work should look like.

Help students form a main idea and write a synthesis of their conclusions.

Assess and Extend

If students are just learning about drawing conclusions…

▶ **USE THE DRAWING CONCLUSIONS TOOL** To work specifically on drawing conclusions, use the **Drawing Conclusions Organizer** in *Tools and Texts.* This tool reinforces the almost mathematical formula for drawing conclusions: find two to three important pieces of information about the subject and, based on those details, draw a conclusion.

If students need to work on their writing skills…

▶ **EVALUATE AND DISCUSS STUDENTS' PARAGRAPHS** If students do a good job drawing the conclusions but need to work on the paragraph, cull strong examples from today's work and put them on an overhead transparency to discuss next time. Explain why these examples are effective. Then have students revise what they wrote, or move on to new material that provides a fresh opportunity to draw conclusions and write.

The **Drawing Conclusions Organizer** tool can be found on the CD-ROM.

If students are ready to extend the lesson…

▶ **BUILD FLUENCY BY DRAWING CONCLUSIONS FROM A VARIETY OF TEXTS**

Use a variety of texts—newspaper and magazine articles, essays, textbooks, and fiction—over time. Keep copies of the Main Idea Organizer and the Drawing Conclusions Organizer available for students to use on their own.

6 Make Inferences About Deeper Meanings

Readers must be able to use what they know from experience and what they learn as they read to make inferences about the deeper meanings of the text.

Essential Skill Set

▶ **Know** what an inference is and how to make one.

▶ **Decide** what kind of information you are trying to infer.

▶ **Determine** what you already know about the subject.

▶ **Generate** a purpose question (PQ) so you can evaluate the information.

▶ **Identify** and apply what you learn to what you already know.

Frame the Lesson

STUDENTS CAN GENERALLY IDENTIFY THE FACTS IN WHAT THEY READ, particularly in informational texts, but many have trouble inferring deeper meanings. While some in-class and state exams pose factual questions, the majority of questions demand more than mere recall; they require students to be able to "read between the lines" or make an inference about cause, importance, meaning, or motive. This lesson describes how to teach students to make inferences and prepare for exams that demand inferential reasoning.

Gather and Prepare

In the model lesson, my students read a short biographical text that is part of our Life Studies unit. The article, "Jesuit Greg Boyle: Gang Priest," is provided in *Tools and Texts*. It includes a simple organizer that helps students make an inference about Father Greg. You can use this simple organizer with any brief article to introduce or review making inferences. See "Assess and Extend" for advanced options.

▶ After reading the model lesson, make notes to adapt the sequence to the article your students will read.

▶ Add the organizer to the article and make copies for each student.

▶ Make an overhead transparency of the article and the organizer.

Shannel highlights key details in the article to help her answer the purpose question. She will then use her notes to complete the inference organizer at the bottom of the page. When she is finished, she will be ready to write an effective paragraph or participate in a discussion.

Teach

HOW CAN I TELL THAT MICHAEL'S FAVORITE TEAM IS THE GIANTS? I'll tell you: *What I already know* is that he has worn something with the Giants' logo on it the last three days; *what I learned* today is that he goes to games and is wearing yet another Giants outfit—so *what I infer* is that Michael is a serious fan and that is his favorite team. *(At this point, Brianna, wearing an LA Dodgers jacket, snaps with good humor, "Dodgers rule!")*

Yes Yessenia, how can I tell that family and friends are very important to you? *(She blushes an "I dunno" and hopes I won't talk about her anymore.)* Well, I noticed you at the beginning of class showing your friends a bunch of photographs from your sister's recent *Quinceanera* celebration and adding them to your binder, which is covered with other family photos. So I take *what I already know* (that your binder has a bunch of wonderful photographs of your family and friends and that you often talk about them), and then I add that to *what I learned* today (that your sister had her big celebration and you are excited about it and want to show the photographs to your friends) and make an inference from that that your family is important to you.

You can think of an inference as an equation, almost like a math equation: "What I learned" plus "what I already know" lets me "make an inference."

What is the difference between an inference and a stereotype?

ANDREW: An inference is a reasonable guess.

So what does it mean to make a "reasonable guess"?

ARIANNA: You have to have some sort of evidence to base your guess on. You can't just take a wild guess; you have to have a reason why you think that.

What happens when you walk into a store like the corner market near school? *(I ask this knowing how they will respond. Immediately they all join in.)*

CLASS: Oh man, they hate kids! They start watchin' you the moment you come in like you're going to steal stuff.

Are they making a "reasonable guess" that you are going to cause trouble or steal?

ONUR: No. They are totally stereotyping you!

Bingo! So let's clarify the difference between an inference and a stereotype. *(After a bit more discussion, we define a stereotype as a guess that has little or no basis, and an inference as a "reasonable" guess based on facts and experience.)*

Let's get down to business now that we have our terms defined. We have been looking at different people's lives as part of our ongoing Life Studies unit this semester. Today we are going to look at the life of a man I respect very much, and we will get to that in a minute. But we also need to keep working on how to read below the surface. In your History class, for example, you get *factual* questions on quizzes about your homework, which you seem to be doing well enough on, but you're having trouble when it comes to the big tests. So we need to keep looking at ways to read more analytically, between the lines. In Health, for example, a quiz will give you a factual question like "What is the most common health disorder among teens in America?" which has only one factual answer. On the exam, however, the question might be, "All of the following are identified as causes of eating disorders EXCEPT…" So you have to puzzle it out. You have to evaluate all the information in that question and decide which choice is not a reasonable response. Today's lesson tries to give you a strategy for how to do such analytical reading using an article about an incredible man named Father Greg Boyle.

I'm going to hand out this article and put a copy up here on the overhead so we can go over this together a bit. That chart at the bottom of the article is an inference organizer. When you make an inference, what you are doing is taking what you already know and adding that to what you learn about the subject from reading. So in this What I Already Know box, we can jot down things you already know about priests. Everyone take a second and do that.

SUSANNA: What if you don't know anything?

You know something about them, even if it's just about how they dress or where they work, right?

MARIO: What if you only know stuff about them from the news? *(He's embarrassed to give more detail but sure that I know what he means.)*

That's okay. Just put down whatever you know.

After they put their own answers down, I solicit some. This gives us a moment to engage in appropriate classroom discussion, something these restless freshmen need to learn and practice. Pooling responses also lets me make sure every student has ideas to work with. I write Joe's responses in the box on the class version of the organizer as an example: "They can't get married, wear certain clothing, and wear that white collar thing."

Good enough! Now we need to set a purpose for ourselves. The article is titled "Jesuit Greg Boyle, Gang Priest." We're reading it as part of our Life Studies unit, so write this PQ—our purpose question—at the top of the handout: "What kind of man is Father Greg Boyle?" *(On another day I might take time to have them develop their own PQ, but giving them the PQ today helps us to focus on the subject of the lesson: making inferences.)*

Now I want you to read the article—it's not that long, actually—and as you do, underline anything in there that will help you answer that question about what kind of a person he is. Remember, what you are doing is preparing to make an inference to figure this out; the article won't tell you outright what kind of a person he is. You have to figure that out by adding what you know about priests to what you learn about him from the article. When you finish, fill in the What the Text Says box. Then use ideas from both columns to make your inference, and write it in the What I Infer… box down below.

Preview the text and identify what students know about the subject.

The article can be found on the CD-ROM.

Generate a purpose question.

Have students read and use the tool to make inferences.

Assess and Extend

If students need practice with academic discussion…

▶ **DISCUSS AND EVALUATE INFERENCES** Have students get into pairs or groups of three or four and share their inferences. If they have significant discrepancies, have them work those out and come up with what they feel is the one best inference about the kind of person Father Greg is.

If students need practice with academic writing…

▶ **WRITE ABOUT THE INFERENCE** Have students use the inference as the basis for a claim about the kind of person Boyle is and then draw on their underlined details to support and illustrate that claim in a paragraph.

If students need to work on test-taking skills…

▶ **GIVE A QUIZ ON INFERENCES** Use the **Inference Quiz** in *Tools and Texts* to follow up on the "Jesuit Greg Boyle" article, or modify it for your text.

If students are ready to make inferences independently…

▶ **USE THE MAKING INFERENCES ORGANIZER** Have students use the **Making Inferences Organizer** (see *Tools and Texts*) with a silent-reading book or other text they are reading on their own. This tool provides space for making three inferences, followed by space to respond and reflect. Students can use their notes to create a focused, organized essay. They can fill in more copies of the tool as they read or create similar charts in their Reader's Notebooks.

The **Inference Quiz** and the **Making Inferences Organizer** can be found on the CD-ROM.

Everything teachers do prepares—or should prepare—students for the work their lives will ask of them. In today's world this means, for example, teaching them to read a variety of texts such as they will encounter as employees, parents, homeowners, and citizens."

–The English Teacher's Companion, p. 8

Analyze the Author's Argument

Identify and analyze the elements used in visual, spoken, and written arguments.

Essential Skill Set

▶ **Determine** the author's purpose.

▶ **Identify** the claim the author makes.

▶ **Evaluate** the reasons and evidence used to persuade the reader.

▶ **Consider** the ethos of the author and the strategies used to persuade.

Frame the Lesson

SOME PEOPLE CLAIM THAT EVERYTHING IS AN ARGUMENT. Every poem, play, story, essay, article, and image is created to persuade the reader or viewer that something is true, important, of a certain quality, or worth doing. Most states now have standards for teaching media literacy so that students can be critical consumers of commercial media, whether it is an advertisement or a political ad. This lesson looks at a written article about the benefits of video games.

Gather and Prepare

The article I use in the model lesson, "Could it be that video games are good for kids?" is provided in *Tools and Texts*. You can use the same strategies and tools with any article that argues for or against an action or presents a point of view. Newspapers and current issues of many magazines are sources for timely, relevant articles. Look for an article that is short enough to put on the overhead, reread, and annotate, all of which are helpful when reading analytically as we are during this lesson.

> ▶ After reading the model lesson, preview the article your students will read. Note anything you want to explain or preview for your kids. Fill in an Argument Organizer for your reference.
>
> ▶ Make copies of the **Argument Organizer** for each student.
>
> ▶ Make copies of the article for each student.
>
> ▶ Provide extra highlighters or colored pencils.

I use the Argument Organizer to keep track of and give structure to what people say as we discuss the article. Sometimes I use the overhead screen; other times I shine the transparency on the whiteboard to allow for more writing space.

⊙ The **Argument Organizer** can be found on the CD-ROM.

Teach

Help kids make connections to arguments and their purpose.

WHAT *IS* AN ARGUMENT? Anyone ever watch old Monty Python shows? Ever see the "Argument Clinic" skit?

> I love that episode, **ARTHUR** *says: (then starts to do a bit of it without prompting)* "Yes, you did…. No, I didn't…. Yes, you did…. No, I didn't…." *(No one else seems to know what he's acting out, but everyone laughs because Arthur is usually quiet.)*

But that is not the kind of argument I am talking about today. I'm talking about the word when it's used, for example, in court or in persuasive writing, as in "the lawyers present their opening arguments," or "in this essay the author argues that the legal driving age should be raised to eighteen." *(This last line draws howls, which is why I use it.)* Oh, you don't like that idea, hey? But if you want to convince someone—legislator, governor, or parent—that it is not a good idea, you must be able to argue your case. You can't just yell or complain; you can't base your argument on a whine or a statement like "but that's so unfair!"—especially when the other side has a pile of statistics about the number of fatal accidents involving drivers under eighteen to present.

So what we are talking about now is how others use language and information to persuade people. Eventually, you will use what we learn here to write your own arguments. For today, though, we are working on how to read arguments, how to analyze them once you see that someone is trying to persuade you.

Connect to a current issue and identify pro and con arguments.

How many of you play video games? How about MySpace.com—how many of you use that? People line up to persuade others of the value and harm of these activities. Who is right? How can we decide? Are video games bad for us—or do they actually have some benefit? Take a second and turn to your neighbor and brainstorm a list of pros and cons for video games. Don't argue with each other about it; just create the list of what people in general say. In other words, the list doesn't have to represent what *you* think.

*The class immediately gets noisy with discussion on both sides of the issue. I spend most of my time nudging kids away from their passionate efforts to convince others and reminding them to just list the pros and cons. When they finish, we take a few minutes to get the ideas on the board, stopping periodically to clarify what someone thinks if they say something that is not clear. **JUSTIN**, for example, says,* "Video games teach you important skills," *so I pause to ask what skills and how they do that. I make it clear I am not challenging him or otherwise doubting him; I just want to help him clarify, then make the point to the class that effective arguments must be clear, precisely stated.*

Analyze an author's argument using the Argument Organizer.

Well, here's an article, written as a letter actually, that argues video games are good for kids. Your parents will no doubt want to call and thank me for having you read this…. If you have a highlighter, it would be useful to have on hand; if not, you can use a crayon out of that can over there. On the overhead I've put up an Argument Organizer, which you should have a copy of, along with a copy of the article. *(I pass out these pages.)*

Help kids identify the author's claim and reason for writing.

The first thing to look for when analyzing an argument is what is called a *claim*. A claim is similar to a thesis. It is the main point you are trying to make. So, to back up: What is the subject of this article, based on a quick scan of it? That's right, video games.

With your highlighter in hand, I want you to read till you find what you think is the claim of this article. In other words, what is Steven Johnson's *argument* about the subject of video games? When you find what you think is his claim, highlight or underline it.

They read, scanning for the claim. I remind them that while it is often stated up front, that is not always the case, as in this article. When I see many students highlighting something, I cut in and ask about it.

Okay, many have highlighted what they think is Johnson's claim. What did you underline?

I highlighted where he says, "In short [video games teach kids] precisely the sorts of skills that they're going to need in the digital workplace of tomorrow," *says* VICTOR, *who seems eager to get home to present this argument to his parents.*

Anyone highlight anything else? Okay, what did you choose?

A few students raise other suggested claims.

Those are definitely related. Do you think Victor's suggestion, which most seem to have chosen, is the one that sums up the main argument in the article? Okay, good. I agree, but why is the claim Victor suggested more effective than your suggestion?

JOE: His is, well, ours is kind of too specific.

Sounds good. The claim Victor suggested covers all the parts of the author's argument, including the part you suggested.

The second key element in any good argument is the *reason* why the person argues for this idea. Sometimes it is sort of integrated into the claim, which this one sort of is, if you look at the line Victor read to us. So, how can we put that claim into the organizer?

With a bit more analysis, we separate the line Victor read into a claim, "Video games are good," and a reason, "because they teach kids precisely the sorts of skills that they're going to need in the digital workplace of tomorrow," to write on the organizer.

What we need to do now is look at the evidence the author uses to support his argument. This is key to any effective argument: you can claim whatever you want, but if you don't offer credible evidence to support it, well, then you won't win the argument. Can anyone tell me what the word *credible* means, by the way?

ELIZABETH: Is it related to credibility?

Yes. So when we say someone "lacks credibility," what do we mean?

ELIZABETH: It means you can't believe what they say.

That's right. And the word *credible* comes from the root that means *belief*—as in the word *credo*, which means what you believe.

Now I want you to go through this article—you can work in small groups if that helps—and find three key pieces of evidence the author provides for his claim.

After they find these, we discuss them, evaluating the credibility of his evidence, and enter them on the organizer.

The last thing—well, two things, really—we will look at today is the idea of acknowledging the other side of the argument. Why is it a good idea to admit the opposing side has some valid points to their argument?

It sort of pulls out the rug on their arguments. It's like in that movie *8 Mile* where Eminem is battling that other dude and Eminem acknowledges that he's white and a rookie and all that stuff that he knows the other dude's gonna bring up. So when the other guy steps up, he doesn't have anything to say, so Eminem wins, *explains* JESSE *who knows all things related to rap.*

Evaluate the author's evidence.

Discuss the importance of acknowledging the other side of an argument.

Oh, that is a fine example, Mr. Cardoza.

So I want you to get in there and find the places where Steven Johnson recognizes that there are bad aspects of video games and then jot those examples down in the Acknowledge section. If you can, find a specific quotation and put that in your notes.

I give them five minutes to do this before we enter their ideas on the class organizer on the overhead.

So we come to the last part: Response. This doesn't have to be big, but it's important because it is the last chance to drive home your argument. This is the "yes–but" section of the argument where, after acknowledging that the other side has a point, you drive home your final points to finish your argument. We have barely enough time to get this done. Skim back over the article—you would expect to find the response toward the end, right? Find the summary of the argument and jot that down.

Assess and Extend

▶ **EVALUATE THE AUTHOR'S ARGUMENT** If students don't finish the Argument Organizer in class, let them finish it at home. To that homework, whether they finished or not, add the requirement that they evaluate how effective the author's argument is. Remind them that their evaluation is also an argument: they are making a claim for or against the effectiveness of Johnson's argument, and they need to support their argument with evidence from the article.

▶ **EXPAND THE ANALYSIS TO CONSIDER ETHOS** Before or after students write their evaluation, you can extend this lesson to address ethos. I define *ethos* as the image of the author that is conveyed in the claim and supporting details. Then I ask, "How do we know we can believe what an author says?" and we list criteria such as these: Is the claim logical? Is the argument thorough? Does the author establish credibility? Do his sources have integrity? Students can use the handout **Understanding Arguments: An Overview** to consider ethos and the strategies used to persuade.

▶ **ANALYZE AN OPPOSING ARGUMENT** Give students another article (ideally one that is against video games, for example) and ask them to independently apply the skills they learned in this lesson.

▶ **EXPAND STUDY AND ANALYSIS OF ARGUMENTS** If students are working on this lesson as part of a larger unit on argument that will culminate in writing a persuasive essay, have them use the Argument Organizer and the handout Understanding Arguments: An Overview to guide them.

(margin notes, left column:)

If students are ready to use their notes to write an analysis…

If students are ready for deeper analysis of the author's argument…

If students show a solid understanding of the elements of an argument…

If students are preparing to write a persuasive essay…

 The **Argument Organizer** tool and the **Understanding Arguments: An Overview** handout can be found on the CD-ROM.

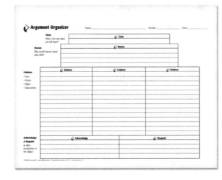

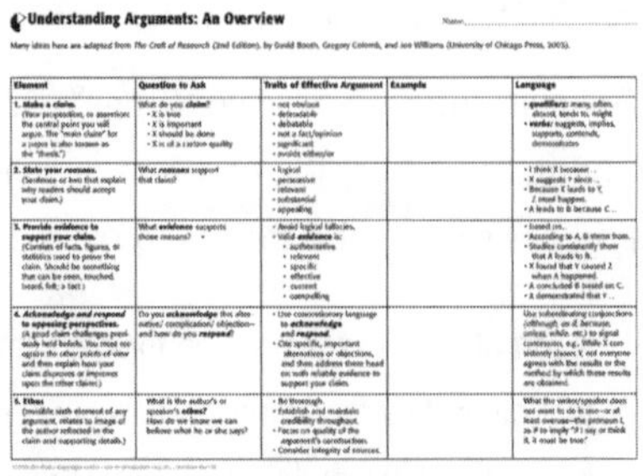

> *We are a practical people who, at least in expository writing, want the author to 'get to the point.' Yet most authors, whether writing fiction or nonfiction, convey many ideas they think are important. Strong readers can sift through stacks of ideas contained in an article or chapter and identify those that are most important, and explain why.*
>
> *—Reading Reminders,* p. 298

8 Examine the Author's Purpose

Effective readers determine and analyze the author's purpose.

Essential Skill Set

▶ **Identify** the author's subject in the text.

▶ **Analyze** what the author says or accomplishes regarding this subject.

▶ **Determine** what rhetorical strategies the author uses and how they help to achieve the author's purpose.

Frame the Lesson

STUDENTS READ MORE NONFICTION NOW THAN IN THE PAST; increasing pressure from universities further drives the demand that students learn how to read rhetorically. As communication becomes more visual, rhetorical strategies also become more evident in ads and other commercial communication. This lesson focuses on a *Time* magazine article in which the author explains why Bruce Lee is one of the most influential people of the 20th century.

Gather and Prepare

In the model lesson, my students read Joel Stein's article "The Time 100: Bruce Lee." The text of this article is provided in *Tools and Texts*. The original article, including the photo and time line, is available online. You can apply the sequence and tools in this lesson to any article or text in which the author uses a rhetorical strategy.

▶ After reading the model lesson, identify and examine the author's purpose in the text your students will read. Using the Academic Writing handout, note the rhetorical strategies that the author uses and mark examples in the text. Fill in a Rhetorical Note**s** tool for reference.

▶ Make copies of the **Academic Writing** handout and the **Rhetorical Notes** tool for each student. Make an overhead transparency of the tool.

▶ Make copies of the "The Time 100: Bruce Lee" article or your text for each student.

José examines an article for rhetorical strategies.

💿 The **Academic Writing** handout and the **Rhetorical Notes** tool can be found on the CD-ROM.

Teach

Help students connect to examining an author's purpose.

TODAY WE ARE TALKING ABOUT THE AUTHOR'S PURPOSE and how authors try to achieve that purpose. No one writes or communicates without some purpose, would you agree? What are advertisements trying to accomplish, for example?

PEDRO: They try to convince you to buy their product.

Of course, and they pay people who can do that big bucks if they are good at it. We'll start a list on the board here to keep track of what we are saying. Everyone should jot down these notes as we go.

On the board I write the heading Purposes *and under it a bullet point •* Persuade.

The question is, *How* do they persuade us? Are there techniques they use?

SELVANNA: They try to make you feel like this product will solve some problem you have.

I add • Problem-Solution *to the list on the board.*

Purposes
• Persuade
• Problem – Solution

Good. There are other things writers try to accomplish, though, aren't there? I know this is new stuff to you in some ways. We have talked about it but not given these strategies names. This Academic Writing sheet that I'm handing out now is a summary of the rhetorical modes that writers (and speakers) use to accomplish their purpose. There are other ways they accomplish it, also. For now, let's work with these as we look at this article about Bruce Lee. While I pass out the article, skim this summary of rhetorical modes.

I pass out the Academic Writing handout, the article, and the Rhetorical Notes tool; then I put a transparency of the tool on the overhead projector.

Preview the article and identify the subject.

Everyone take a minute to preview the article. What should you look at when previewing—also sometimes called skimming—the article?

STUDENTS *give various responses:* Bold words. The title. The headings.

Yes, these are all good to look at. Anything else? ... No? Look at this Bruce Lee article. What else might we run our eyes over for a second to get some info?

The photographs, *suggests* **ROFIDA,** *sounding a bit unsure of herself.*

Of course! Are images used to achieve some purpose? Of course: sometimes they are used to persuade, others to illustrate or offer a visual comparison. Anything else we should look at? What about that thing under the photograph? What do you call that?

BEN: The caption.

Yes. Anything else we should look at, Ben?

BEN: The time line at the bottom. That emphasizes the main events in Lee's life. And that thing at the top—I don't know what you call that.

Oh, that. That's called a "pull quote." Yes, that's great. It is usually a sentence that sums up some key idea in the article. Books don't tend to do that.

Use the Rhetorical Notes tool to analyze what Stein says about Bruce Lee.

So on the Rhetorical Notes tool, in the Subject area, what can we write down?

JAMIL: Bruce Lee.

Now you are going to read it, the whole article, to figure out what his claim—the main point the writer wants to make—is *about* Bruce Lee. In this particular article, however, there is an extra bit of help. This article was part of a special edition of *Time* magazine titled *Time 100*, the 100 most important people of the 20th century.

So in that second box you could write the beginning of your claim like this: "Joel Stein argues that Bruce Lee…." You have to figure out how to complete that sentence…read to figure out *why* Bruce Lee is in *Time 100* and what he did that is so important.

They read, and I walk around after quickly reviewing my own notes so I am prepared to provide support. When they are finished or finishing, I call them back together.

What are some different ways we could complete that sentence about the main idea, or claim, of the article? *(On the overhead, I write, "Joel Stein argues that Bruce Lee…" and wait to write down the list of possible completions. We discuss a few, each of which I write down as the students suggest them.)*

Which of these most effectively addresses the author's purpose? What is Stein trying to accomplish here?

MICHAEL: He is trying to explain why Bruce Lee is so important, how he changed the film industry.

Yes, that's true. So is his purpose to "explain," or is it something more specific? Look at the list of rhetorical modes on the Academic Writing sheet I gave you earlier, and figure out which one best captures the author's purpose here.

ELIZABETH: He's trying to persuade readers.

Of what? How can you tell? *(I want her to elaborate on and defend her answer.)*

ELIZABETH: Well, he says how so many things changed because of Bruce Lee, not just in movies but like where it talks about the interest in health and fitness. So he is trying to convince us that Bruce Lee started that, so he's important not just because of his movies but because of the impact he had on society overall.

Way to go, Elizabeth! Good response. You provided examples to support what you said and identified the heart of Stein's argument.

So what can we say about his claim? Let's state it this way on the tool: "Joel Stein argues that Bruce Lee not only created opportunities for Chinese actors but changed the way Americans think about themselves and their bodies."

Huddle up now and find three key points—quotations or examples—you can add to that third box that the author, Stein, uses to support his claim or achieve his purpose. Elizabeth already gave us some good ideas.

If this is the first time I am using this tool or introducing this idea, we will come back together and discuss the different points. If not—if they understand it all—we will move on to focus on the discussion of the text instead of the author's purpose and techniques.

Everyone seems to be doing a pretty good job of working through this. I want you to take what you have so far and finish it up for homework tonight. We need to work through these things individually; you don't always get to collaborate when you read or write. When you come in tomorrow, I will expect you to have the rest of the Rhetorical Notes sheet completed.

Develop students' academic language, giving them prompts if necessary.

Use the Academic Writing handout to identify Stein's strategy.

Identify the traits of successful responses.

Have students complete the Rhetorical Notes for homework.

Assess and Extend

**If students need
more support...**

▶ **GUIDE COMPLETION OF THE RHETORICAL NOTES** If students need additional
support, don't have them finish the tool at home. Instead, work through each step,
modeling and, if necessary, allowing them to collaborate on each step. Then follow
up with more independent practice with subsequent articles.

**If students need to work
on summarizing...**

▶ **EVALUATE STUDENTS' SUMMARIES** Have students hand in their summaries. (See the
bottom of the Rhetorical Notes tool.) Copy examples of strong performances, and put
each example on the overhead to analyze what works in the summary.

Summarize the author's argument, focusing on the subject, purpose, and rhetorical strategies used to achieve that purpose.

Continue on the back

The **Rhetorical Notes** tool can be found on the CD-ROM.

**If students need to practice
academic discussion...**

▶ **USE THE RHETORICAL NOTES TOOL TO FACILITATE DISCUSSION** Have students use
their Rhetorical Notes to participate in a discussion the following day, returning to the
text to find examples to support and refine their observations.

9 Visualize What You Read

Effective readers use details from the text to visualize what it means.

Essential Skill Set

▶ **Locate** and use sensory and spatial details to create a "movie in your head" as you read.

▶ **Evaluate** which details are most important to the meaning of the text.

▶ **Assess** and investigate details you cannot "see" and thus cannot understand until you get more information.

Frame the Lesson

WHETHER READING POETRY OR LITERATURE, TEXTBOOKS ABOUT DISTANT CULTURES, or articles about current events, all students struggle at times to make sense of what they read. Often, even advanced students lack the background knowledge needed to identify and use the visual information contained—directly or indirectly—in figures of speech or expository prose about people, places, events, or ideas. To develop this skill, readers at all levels must learn how to identify such details, evaluate which ones matter most, generate images using those details, and fill in the blanks when they don't know what something means. This lesson shows them how to visualize while reading a sonnet. Kids at all levels find sonnets elusive, often because they simply can't picture what the poet is describing.

Gather and Prepare

Shakespeare's Sonnet 116, which we read in the model sequence, and Sonnet 18 in "Assess and Extend" are standard English class texts. You can find them in *Tools and Texts* or adapt the sequence to any text that is rich in imagery.

▶ After reading the model lesson, preview the text you will teach. Annotate the imagery. Note repeated or thematic ideas, such as the "fixed" and "changing" images in Sonnet 116. Make a chart to organize your notes.

▶ Make copies of the sonnet or your text for each student.

▶ Prepare an overhead transparency of the text.

Michelle assesses her comprehension of Sonnet 116 by highlighting the parts she does not understand before huddling up with other students to find visual details to improve their understanding. Throughout the reading process, students pause frequently to evaluate their performance.

Help kids connect to
visualizing as a
way to improve
understanding.

Teach

WE ARE GOING TO BE READING A SHAKESPEARE PLAY SOON, but before we launch into that, I want to get us warmed up. I find kids can learn to read Shakespeare well, but they often find it difficult at first because they don't know what things look like as they are reading. It's similar to reading an ancient text like *The Odyssey,* when you read about the hall in which people eat, sing, fight, and so on. Not too much like what your home looks like or any place you've been to unless you've done some serious traveling. I've seen my share of castles, for example, so I can draw on that experience when I want to "see" what is going on in some of these older plays and epics.

Back in Shakespeare's day, people knew what he was describing. And of course his plays were performed for an audience—they still are, as you know. But when you're reading, you have to visualize everything, like making a movie in your head. And it's not just places that give you trouble sometimes, is it? What are some other things that get in the way of your understanding what Shakespeare, for example, is talking about?

ANNA: He uses all sorts of funny words.

ARTHUR: Yeah, sometimes they are words I know, but he uses them in a way that makes no sense to me. I can't think of an example, but you see that a lot in his plays.

I know what you mean. Today I want to show you how to work through that kind of stuff with a poem, one of his sonnets. I'm not going to tell you what it means, but instead I want you to focus on *how* to read it and figure out *how* it means what it does on your own. What do I mean by figuring out "*how* it means"? Good question, huh... The quick answer is that if I tell you *what* it means, you'll know what that one poem means but not how Shakespeare created that meaning. What's more, you will come to the next poem without any sense of how to approach it. But if I show you *how* it means what it does, you can get a foot on the ladder and climb into the poem, break into the house, as it were, all on your own.

Everyone has a copy of Sonnet 116, or you should. The first thing I want you to do is read through the poem, underlining anything you don't understand. When you finish, give yourself a score of 1 to 10, 1 meaning you have NO idea what that poem was about, 10 meaning you understand it better than Shakespeare himself. Then take a minute to explain why you gave yourself the score you did.

They read, score, and write.

Anyone get a 10? *(To which they respond with moans and "No way!")*

Have students locate and use
details to create a mental
"movie."

Huddle up with a partner and go through the poem and just look for things you can "see" or picture in your mind. For example, "tempests"—what's that? Right, tempests are storms. What about a "wandering bark"? Ah, a bit tougher. Get out some dictionaries and get in there. Don't assume that you know what it is just because you know the word.

As they settle in, I move around to question their ideas. When they read a word such as compass, for example, they want to assume they know what it means; I push them to get into the dictionary and think of other, more visual possibilities. Ross, Meghan, Jason, and Lourdes are lost on a line I know others will struggle with. Before I settle in to work with them a bit, I move to the board and draw a two-column, T-shape, diagram for the class.

Sonnet 116

Sonnet 116
William Shakespeare

Let me not to the marriage of true minds
Admit impediments. Love is not love
Which alters when it alteration finds,
Or bends with the remover to remove:
O no! it is an ever-fixed mark
That looks on tempests and is never shaken;
It is the star to every wandering bark,
Whose worth's unknown, although his height be taken.
Love's not Time's fool, though rosy lips and cheeks
Within his bending sickle's compass come:
Love alters not with his brief hours and weeks,
But bears it out even to the edge of doom.
   If this be error and upon me proved,
   I never writ, nor no man ever loved.

Everyone, look up here a minute and try this to get into the imagery a bit deeper. Make a T-chart on your paper. Write *Change* at the top of the left column, and go through the sonnet and look for details that have something to do with changing. In this column, list all the words related to things that change or are not stable, "tempests," for example. Label the other column *Fixed*, and list those words, such as "ever fixéd mark," that suggest something is immovable, permanent, or unchanging.

(I return to Ross' group.) Okay, let's look at these lines that are stumping you. First, realize that everyone else feels the same way, okay? Here they are:

> Love's not Time's fool, though rosy lips and cheeks
>
> Within his bending sickle's compass come.

Let's ask some questions and figure out what those lines are saying so you can get a picture in your head. Why is *Time* capitalized? Right, because it's being personified. Good word to use there. Make a note that says that Time is personified. Now if *Love* was not the first word, do you think it would still be capitalized—and if so, why?

LOURDES: Yes, it would be, because "rosy lips and cheeks" refers to Love. *(Everyone in her group shows the proper awe and respect for this insight.)*

What about that pronoun *his*—what's that referring to?

ROSS: That's what we don't get.

What does Time look like when it's personified? Are there other names for Time?

MEGHAN: Oh, I know. It's like the—what do you call that thing? The Grim Reaper, right? It's an old man in a hood, and he's got that blade thing, the sickle.

Good! Now what about *compass?* How does that relate to Time and the sickle? I'll give you a hint: What is that on the wall over there? That's right—the clock. So what *is* a compass? Sure, it's what you use to guide yourself. But don't you use one in your geometry class, too? If you look up *compass* in the dictionary, you'll find a definition that emphasizes the shape, the roundness of something like a clock.

So make these lines into a movie in your mind. Imagine I'm Time, standing here with my "sickle." Now if "rosy lips and cheeks"—why are they "rosy" by the way? Right, because they are *alive*—within my "bending sickle's compass come" (picture my sickle like the hands of the clock moving in a circle, cutting down one minute after another). Then what is Shakespeare saying about love?

LOURDES: I get it. He's saying that people all die, but love is not something you can kill.

Riiiiight! You've got it! Now see what you can visualize in the next lines and add to that movie in your head and your T-chart.

I move on, going from group to group until I sense that most are ready to wrap up.

Everyone's had time to wrestle with this. Now I want you to read the poem through again, by yourself, thinking about what your group discussed. I want you to give yourself a new score of 1 to 10. This time, instead of explaining your score, I want you to explain what you did that improved your understanding: what strategies you used and what questions you asked, especially those you could use to help you understand other poems.

Make a chart to evaluate details that are important to the meaning.

Model how to assess and investigate details they don't understand.

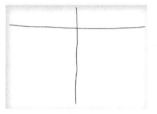

Have students make a T-chart to help them organize their thoughts.

Assess and Extend

If students need more support…

▶ **REVIEW AND VISUALIZE THE TEXT TOGETHER** If there are parts of the poem that students still do not understand, take the time to discuss them, letting those in the class who figured them out do the explaining. For example, the group I worked with can now guide others through the "Time" image and explain how they used the details to visualize what it meant.

If students need to practice their writing skills…

▶ **WRITE TO SYNTHESIZE THE IMAGES** To work on writing, have students synthesize their notes in a well-organized paragraph that explains how Shakespeare uses visual details in the poem to support his assertion that real love is unchanging, steady.

If students are ready to practice visualizing on their own…

▶ **VISUALIZE A TEXT INDEPENDENTLY** To develop their ability to visualize, have students repeat this sequence using Sonnet 18 and come in the next day prepared to explain how Shakespeare uses visual details, and how they used them to figure out the poem's meaning.

If students enjoy or benefit from expressing ideas artistically…

▶ **DRAW WHAT IS BEING VISUALIZED** Instead of writing, have students draw what they visualized in the sonnet. They might create images in sequence, section by section, or find other ways of representing the images and meanings in the text. See **Visualizing Strategies** in *Tools and Texts*.

 The **Visualizing Strategies** tool can be found on the CD-ROM.

“ *Incorporate into the study of literature a range of texts of different types and perspectives, in different media, so that through this breadth of material students may learn about and participate in the larger conversation about the literary tradition.”*

—The English Teacher's Companion, p. 64

10 Examine Multiple Perspectives

Compare different perspectives on the same character, event, idea, or experience as represented through different media using words, images, and graphics.

Essential Skill Set

▶ **Analyze** language and its equivalent elements in different media.

▶ **Evaluate** the composition of elements in an artist's interpretation.

▶ **Examine** the artist's choices and how those contribute to the interpretation.

▶ **Compare** artists' perspectives with the corresponding text.

Frame the Lesson

WE WANT KIDS TO BE ABLE TO VIEW A SUBJECT FROM MANY SIDES and through different media. This demands critical reading and viewing skills, including the ability to compare elements in different productions. While it is essential for students to consider a subject from the perspectives of different characters in the text, they should also be able to analyze how these subjects are treated in different media in order to improve their "textual intelligence," that is, their ability to understand a text on many levels (Burke 2001). In this lesson my class looks at paintings of Ophelia, a main character in Shakespeare's *Hamlet,* to examine three artists' interpretations. As an extension, we compare Ophelia scenes from different film productions of *Hamlet.* Many literary works have been interpreted in art, film, theater, and music. You can adapt this lesson to examine any subject for which you can provide two or more interpretations.

Gather and Prepare

A Web search using the character name, title, author, and media form you are seeking will turn up resources to use in your classroom. For example, entering keywords "Ophelia *Hamlet* paintings" will bring up resources for the model lesson, including The Ophelia Page.

▶ Locate at least two artworks or film scenes for the novel or play your class is reading. Obtain copies in a form you can present in class.

▶ After reading the model lesson, reflect on the interpretations you have chosen. Prepare a comparison chart as described in the model lesson and use it to note points you want to cover.

▶ Prepare a list of text references that correspond to the interpretations.

A student consults the text of *Hamlet* while looking for quotations to correspond with details from the paintings. Note the organizer laid out in three columns for three perspectives on Ophelia.

Teach

EVERY DAY WHILE DRIVING HOME, I LISTEN TO *The NewsHour with Jim Lehrer*, a news show that examines a few key issues in depth. What I love about it is the way that it gathers different people from a range of fields and perspectives and has them discuss a subject about which they are all experts. It reminds me, as I listen to one perspective after another, each different yet related, that there are always other ways to view a subject. It's like when a bank gets robbed and the police ask people what happened: the reports can be so distinctive that each witness seems to have seen an entirely different event. So it is with stories and ideas, as we each read them through the filters of our own perspective, our own experiences, and our own culture.

You see this done in fascinating ways with Shakespeare's plays. Every time *Hamlet* is put on, you get a different Hamlet, a new Ophelia. One Ophelia might be utterly mad, another strident, a third frail and sad. It's interesting—and useful—to consider how others view a subject, how others tell the same story in a different way to support their interpretation. Artists and actors all put their own spin on characters. Today we are going to examine how different artists see Ophelia and interpret her death. She is a popular subject of artists, and you can find many paintings of her on the Web. I chose three for us to look at today. The first is *Ophelia* by John Everett Millais, painted in 1852 and probably the most famous painting of Ophelia. Then we will look at *Ophelia* by Arthur Hughes, painted 1851–1853, and *Ophelia* by John William Waterhouse from 1894. Waterhouse actually painted several versions of Ophelia, each quite different, but we'll look at just one of his versions today.

Before I show you the first painting, divide a sheet of paper into three columns with these titles at the top: Ophelia by Millais, Ophelia by Hughes, and Ophelia by Waterhouse. *(Sometimes I use the Three-Column Organizer tool for this assignment.)*

Here is Millais' *Ophelia*. As you can see, she's dead, floating in water. But examine this image carefully and see what else you notice. Jot down words and phrases that describe what you see, words that describe both the painting and the artist's technique. For example, note how Ophelia's hands are positioned. What words could you use to describe that gesture? And notice how the artist uses light: What parts of the image are

Ophelia by John Everett Millais, Tate Gallery, London.

bright, and what parts are dark? What tone or feeling does the painting convey? What words come to mind to characterize this Ophelia?

Now take a look at the other two paintings. Both artists show Ophelia alive, just before her death, but the perspectives are different. As you examine each image, make sure you evaluate the same elements; for example:

- Pay attention to the use of light and the arrangement of her body.

- Focus on the tone in each one, and think about what the artists used instead of words to create that tone.

- What words come to mind to characterize each of these Ophelias?

I spend ten to fifteen minutes directing students' attention to particular details and helping them generate the language needed to complete the task, as this is a new way of working to many of them. It also provides a context in which to discuss tone and characterization, so I want to give some emphasis to those terms.

Before we talk about what you think, take a moment to compare what others came up with when looking at the same images. If someone saw something you didn't, ask them to explain that and what they think it means, why it's important. If you are convinced it is a viable interpretation, add it to your notes.

Examine other perspectives.

As they talk, I move from group to group to see what they came up with but also to get some examples to refer to when I move ahead. If I see some great work from students who might not normally speak up, I will call on them knowing that they have something to be proud of and will set them up to succeed.

Now get into the text and find the passage in Act 4, Scene 7, in which Gertrude describes Ophelia's death. Find specific words in the passage and add those to your notes, especially those details that connect to each artist's rendering. Can you find lines that correspond with one painting or another or fit a particular detail in a painting?

Have students analyze the corresponding text.

I give students time to read the passage and add details to their notes.

Okay, so you've looked at different paintings, compared them to the play's text, and shared your ideas with each other. Sounds like you are ready to write. But I don't want some rambling freewrite; I want a paragraph with a specific focus, a point it is trying to prove about Ophelia. And I want you to use details from the paintings and *Hamlet* itself to support what you say. Before you begin, let's quickly brainstorm some words on the board that you might use to make effective comparisons while writing this paragraph.

Prepare to write.

I list words on the board as kids call them out; if a word is vague or questionable, I pose questions to help students clarify and get a better word. Then I give everyone time to write until the bell is about to ring.

Everyone seems to be finished, and we are running out of time. Hang on to this paragraph because tomorrow I will show you a couple of versions of the Ophelia scene from films so we can see how different directors and actors interpret her character. We will add those details to our notes, and then you will incorporate them into a character analysis of Ophelia, in which you will use quotations and examples from these different interpretations to support and illustrate your claim about her character.

Assess and Extend

If you have access to different versions of the play or story on video…

▶ **EXAMINE FILM OR STAGE PRODUCTIONS** Extend or vary the lesson by showing different dramatic interpretations of the text or of scenes from the text. Set up a similar page of two- or three-column notes and follow the same instructional sequence except for videos. (Refer to Lesson 40: Take Notes from Videos.)

If students need support or practice with examining characterization…

▶ **ANALYZE CHARACTERIZATION** Use this assignment as an example of what the students should do when analyzing a character; then have them choose another main character and study that character. (Refer to Lesson 14: Analyze Character Development.)

If students need more support for understanding the text…

▶ **ANALYZE THE TEXT** If we need to work inside the text more—i.e., not go outside to other media or sources, which is a more advanced task—I use **Target Notes** or the **Conversational Roundtable**. In either of these tools, I have students write "Ophelia" in the center. Then, depending on their level of ability, we fill in the other areas on the organizer with the names of other characters in the text. We begin with the obvious: Hamlet and Polonius, Ophelia's father, and examine how they view Ophelia. If students are ready, we include more characters and examine how each of them views Ophelia. Should we have the time and will for one more level of complexity, we add Ophelia herself, taking notes to explain how she sees herself. Once we finish the organizer, we use it as the basis for a carefully structured piece of writing, complete with quotations and commentary that support our claim about Ophelia. You can use either of these tools to help kids analyze other literary texts.

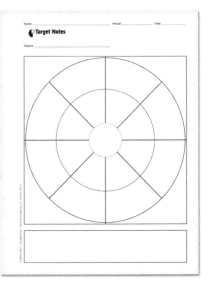

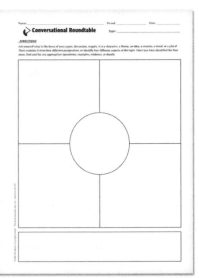

The **Target Notes** and the **Conversational Roundtable** tools can be found on the CD-ROM.

*The most important capacities we can develop in our students are the belief in the value of reading and their ability to read any text they encounter…. Develop students' story grammar by examining—through analysis, manipulation, and comparison/ contrast—different examples (e.g., linear, collage, flashback, narrative leaps or what filmmakers call "cutaways") and how they affect meaning, how they work."

–Reading Reminders pp. 234 and 292

11 Examine the Structure of a Text

Effective readers analyze the organizational structure of a text to understand how it contributes to the meaning of that text.

Essential Skill Set

▶ **Identify** the key junctures and patterns throughout the text.

▶ **Analyze** how those events or details are arranged.

▶ **Draw** conclusions about why the author organized those details that way.

Arthur and O'Brian work with members of their group to gather details about different stages of the novel as they study its organizational structure to see how the story unfolds.

Frame the Lesson

UNDERSTANDING ORGANIZATIONAL PRINCIPLES IS CENTRAL to understanding both literary and informational texts. When reading literature, students cannot understand the plot if they do not understand how events are organized and how that organizational structure contributes to the meaning of the story as a whole. Some text structures are straightforward, while others are complex. We expect students to develop the necessary skills to understand increasingly complex or subtle text structures. While it is equally important to know how to analyze informational text structure, this lesson focuses on how the plot of a novel is organized. It's essential for readers to understand that writers build stories in different ways for particular reasons.

Gather and Prepare

In the model lesson, my students analyze the structure of Joseph Conrad's novel *Heart of Darkness*. As we work through the novel, I help them identify locations that are essential to the main events of the plot. For each location, they answer a set of questions that help them see how those settings form a structure for the novel. You can use a similar sequence for other novels or texts that have multiple settings across time.

▶ After reading the model lesson, think about the novel you are teaching. Jot down key locations or major events that form the spine of the story. Use these notes to plan and implement your lesson.

▶ Decide whether you will create a chart on the board, as I do in the model lesson, or use a different organizer. See "Assess and Extend" for options.

▶ Make planning notes to adapt the model lesson to your class.

▶ Put your organizer on the board or a transparency to fill in together.

Teach

Make connections between text structure and meaning.

WE ARE JUST BEGINNING TO READ *Heart of Darkness,* but already some of you are finding it confusing, which is natural as it is a difficult book. I thought that we would work on how the story is organized since that can help you understand what is going on as you read the rest of the book. Getting some sort of a sense of how a text "works" allows you to make predictions and better understand how one thing relates to another. It's sort of like a map: we all need some sense of the big picture to see how it all fits together.

You're going to need two full pages in your Reader's Notebook to do this. Take a second to copy down the chart I have on the board. *(Before class I drew the following spreadsheet on the whiteboard.)*

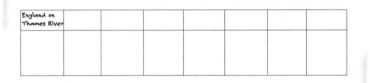

Identify key junctures and patterns throughout the text.

As you read through the book, I want you to figure out the seven key locations or set-tings for the story. The first one takes place on the boat in London where the charac-ters describe themselves on the Thames River. In the coming days I will help you to figure out what the other key locations are, though you should take notes about what you think are the key settings as you read. Get together with a small group to talk about what you've read so far. Note key events and details that occur in the first loca-tion and tell why you think these are important.

They set about drawing the organizer and discussing the opening scenes in the book. As I circle around to monitor, I won't correct but will ask questions like, "That's an important detail, but isn't it part of a bit larger scene in the book? What happens just before that? Go back to the book to take a look."

Write to analyze the first key juncture and what it represents.

Okay, most of you are finished, and if you aren't, you've done some serious thinking about the first location and are ready to discuss it. Before we do that, however, let's take a few minutes and write a short paragraph in your Reader's Notebook in which you make a claim about what this stage of the book represents. Don't summarize it, but be sure to include some examples from the book to support and illustrate your point.

They write in their notebooks for about five minutes.

Let's compare what you all came up with by way of discussing this first location in the novel. Even if you have something different than we come up with, that's fine because when you get new ideas, it helps you see why the old ones weren't quite right.

We build the organizer on the whiteboard fairly quickly, talking about what happened to whom and how that "contributes to the meaning of the story" at this point. As kids call out details they think are crucial to the first location, I ask them such questions as, "Why do you think that is an important aspect of the opening?"

The point here is to set up the notes so you can study how the book unfolds as you read and get a sense of the order of events that take place in these different locations and how the movement and events from one place to the next contribute to the mean-ing of the story. You read the whole chapter for homework last night, so you should be able to turn your attention to the second column in the graph. Begin by identifying the second key location and preparing a rationale for why that setting is so distinct. Then go ahead and discuss that location as you did the first one on the chart, jotting down details in that column that answer these questions *(which I write on the board):*

- Who is involved in the scene?

- What are these people doing in that scene?

- How is that scene described (in detail, taking quotations from the book)?

- What changed in this location compared to the one before it? Changes apply to the people (for example, do their feelings about themselves or their situation change), the setting, or the plot.

- Why does it change—and why is that change important?

As you talk about these first two locations, try to pay close attention to how things change. This is important in helping you understand the book and how it's organized because this book does not have many chapters, unlike other books. So within one chapter you could have three important scenes but nothing helps to really announce those changes. You have to learn to see these junctures or key moments yourself.

They go back to work, discussing the rest of the chapter to find other key scenes; the work carries over to the next day. As they work, I pose questions to challenge what they put down. For example, I will ask, "How is the Central Station different from the Outer Station?" And after a bit of talk, I might further ask, "How does Conrad describe the Central Station? Yes, you're right, much more chaotic, much more emphasis on how dark everything is. So what purpose do that chaos and darkness serve—how do they contribute to the book's meaning?" I am not giving them answers but modeling the questions they must learn to ask to come up with the answers themselves when reading this or any other novel.

Most are finished with this, so let me cut in and tell you what to do next so you can jump to this when you are ready. We've been working on our analytical writing, specifically on how one thing causes or leads to another and how those events contribute to the meaning of the text in a poem or a story. What I want you to do now is use this wonderfully organized chart you have created as an outline for an extended paragraph that explains how the book is organized. Don't summarize the story, but analyze its organization and how that contributes to the meaning. Here is *one* way to begin. You can use, adapt, or ignore this—it's just a suggestion:

Joseph Conrad organizes *Heart of Darkness* to show how people change the farther they are from their own civilization.

I give kids time to write until near the end of class.

If you are finished, that's great. Hang on to your writing so we can work with it some more tomorrow. If you need more time, take it home and finish it up.

Use questions to analyze how events and details are arranged.

Have students identify and analyze other key junctures.

Draw conclusions and write about why the author organized the text this way.

Assess and Extend

If students need to work on academic discussion...

▶ **USE THE CHART AND THEIR WRITING TO FACILITATE DISCUSSION** This helps struggling students and English language learners who have a hard time with spontaneous discussions but can, if they are prepared, contribute to the discussion.

If students need to work on expository writing skills...

▶ **USE THIS WRITING ASSIGNMENT TO FOCUS ON SOME ASPECT OF WRITING THAT IS IMPORTANT TO THEIR SUCCESS** In this case, for example, students can work on transitions. Have them highlight the transition words they have used. If there aren't many, have them rework their paragraphs and find the places they should have transitions. Brainstorm words they can use at different junctures to provide organization in their paper about the organization in the story.

If students are ready to examine a variety of organizational structures...

▶ **EXTEND THE LESSON** The tools include the following options for examining organizational structures and techniques:

- The **Plot Notes** tool uses the classical triangle shape to examine exposition, rising action, climax, falling action, and resolution.

- The **Narrative Design** tool examines narrative elements such as digression and flashback to see how they contribute to primary events.

- **Time Line Notes** help readers sequence events and examine cause and effect relationships in literary and informational texts.

- The **Organizational Patterns** handout describes eight organizational patterns that may be found in narrative, expository, or persuasive text. It includes signal words for reading and writing about each pattern.

Plot Notes, Narrative Design, Time Line Notes, and **Organizational Patterns** can be found on the CD-ROM.

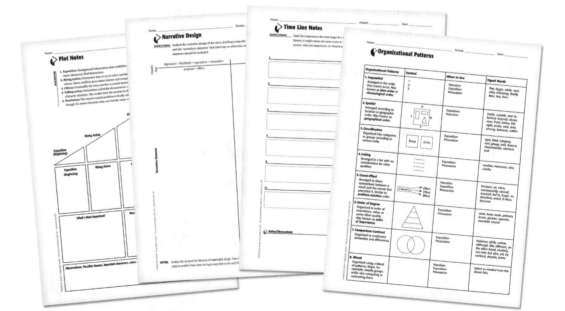

12 Ask Questions About What You Read

Effective readers ask a variety of questions for different reasons when reading.

Essential Skill Set

▶ **Generate** questions that are appropriate to ask about this subject.

▶ **Evaluate** and choose the questions you use based on your purpose.

▶ **Use** your questions to guide your reading and organize your answers.

After generating questions about the essay they have read, students focus on the question they have chosen. Each group will post their questions and answers for all to use for the subsequent class discussion and writing assignment.

Frame the Lesson

WHETHER IN THE WORKFORCE, ON STATE TESTS, OR IN CLASS, students must be able to perform independently those tasks they are assigned. While they need a range of strategies to use in different situations, students can use questions to begin solving nearly all academic or intellectual problems. This lesson is based on the idea that students must learn what questions to ask when reading analytically so they can independently solve the problems the text presents. The model lesson shows how to develop questions students can use to analyze and prepare to write about a fictional character.

Gather and Prepare

In the model lesson, I help my students develop questions about characters in Joseph Conrad's novel *Heart of Darkness,* which they are reading for class. Then they work in groups to focus on one character and one question, using the Text Tool to record details from the text to answer their question and make a claim about their subject. You can use the same strategies and tool to explore characters in any class novel or short story. To generate questions for other reasons and other types of text, see "Assess and Extend."

▶ Make copies of the **Text Tool** for each student.

▶ After reading the model lesson, make a list of questions that you want to be sure are included on the class list for the text you are teaching. Note passages you want students to consider. Use your list as a reference and guide.

▶ Similarly, create a T-chart of minor and major characters to anticipate students' ideas. Prepare a sample response using the Text Tool.

▶ Use a tool from "Assess and Extend" if it fits your students' needs.

Get kids thinking about asking their own questions.

Teach

THE OTHER DAY I HEARD A TEACHER SAY SHE HAD REALIZED that without her around, her students didn't know which questions to ask when reading their books or writing their papers. This reminded me of another teacher who once said that he learned more about teaching during the week he had laryngitis than he had in twenty years. My point is that I realized that when you take the state test or walk into college or the workplace down the line, I won't be there—nor should I have to be. You need to know which questions to ask to get the job done and when to ask them. Today we are going to focus on generating questions you can use to help you read this novel well and come out of it ready to write. Once we are done, I want you to work with your reading groups to answer these questions using the Text Tool I will give you later.

On the board I write "Questions to Ask About a Character" and draw a line under it to signal that a list will follow.

Generate appropriate questions to ask about a character.

So what *are* some questions you can ask—I'm not going to give them to you!—to help you understand a character? Remember also that to understand a character is to understand a person. So what questions do you ask to be able to understand another human being?

As kids call them out, we discuss and refine them as needed and then write them on a sheet of butcher paper taped to the board so we can keep and add to our list. We generate the following questions.

> What does the character want, and why does he or she want it?
>
> How do other characters and the author feel about this character?
>
> What role does the character play in the story?
>
> What effect does this character have on others in the story?
>
> What are the most important things to know about this character?

This is a good list; we can add to it if new ideas come to you in the next steps. To prepare for the next step, we need a list of the important characters in the book.

I create a T-chart on the board and write Minor Characters as the left heading and Major Characters as the right heading.

What are some questions we should ask about minor and major characters?

> What is a minor character? *asks* **BILL,** *which I acknowledge is a good question.*
>
> How do you distinguish between a minor and a major character? **ANN** *asks, which I again note is a useful question.*

Distinguish *major* characters from *minor* characters. Generate lists of each.

These are good questions because they force us to define what we mean. Questions should always serve a purpose: to clarify, define, classify, and so on.

Minor Characters	Major Characters

Let's generate a list of characters and then discuss these questions as we classify characters. Who then is a character to put up here?

Minor Characters	Major Characters
The men on the boat	Marlow
The Pilgrims	Kurtz
The Cannibals	The general Manager
	the Brickmaker
	the Accountant
	the Intended

ALLISON: The men on the boat, the ones Marlow is talking to.

Are they minor or major characters?

Minor, *says someone in the back. (I put the characters' names in the Minor column.)*

What makes them minor, though? That is what we need to know. What is a question we can use, one that we can keep in our back pocket to figure that out on our own?

LEILANI: Well, you ask whether things would change if you took that character out of the story. If you can take them out and it doesn't change the story, then they are only minor characters.

ANTONIO: The accountant Marlow meets early on is a major character.

Why do you think that character is so important?

ANTONIO: The accountant had a long talk with Marlow.

RACHEL: But it didn't change anything in the story. The accountant was just a device the author used to represent the kind of people in charge of the company over in Africa.

We build a good list of about eight major characters to work with.

Now get into your reading groups and send someone up to choose the character your group will study; just cross it out and put your name next to it. Then get copies of the Text Tool handout. Look up here to see my example on the overhead. Write your major character in the Subject area of your handout and one of the questions from the list in the Question area. Within your group, you'll have the same character but different questions. Then rub your heads together over the text, and get in there and find evidence in the text, specific examples and quotations you can cite (and which you *will* cite!) for future use when writing. You are looking for details to help you answer your question but also to prepare you to write a response to it.

Have groups choose a question and use it to guide their reading and organize their response.

As they set to work, I move from group to group to coax, clarify, and challenge. They need to work efficiently but also thoughtfully. Some divide up, working individually within the group to complete the Text Tool sheet and only consulting the others for clarification. Others collaborate on one question at a time, working together to find evidence in the text and discussing how that evidence helps to answer the question.

Later, depending on the time needed, the next day, or even two days later…

Now use the notes and quotations you've gathered to write down the answer (as a claim) to focus your question. The notes should support and illustrate your claim if you were to write a paragraph (or more) about this subject.

Allow students to work in different ways to solve the same academic problems.

Assess and Extend

If students need to work on academic discussion…

▶ **EXTEND THE DISCUSSION** Have students complete the Text Tool with a claim that their evidence can support. Then convene the full class and let students use their notes to support their participation in the class discussion.

If students are ready to focus on writing…

▶ **USE THE TEXT TOOL TO WRITE A RESPONSE** Have students use their claim and the notes and quotes from their Text Tool to write a well-organized paragraph with evidence that supports and illustrates the claim. As a related follow-up, have kids enter into a discussion using these paragraphs. For more extended writing, have them write a short paper or what some call an "extended paragraph" on the subject.

If students would benefit from an alternate approach…

▶ **ASK QUESTIONS FOR DIFFERENT PURPOSES AND DIFFERENT TYPES OF TEXTS** These tools include many options for asking questions and helping students generate questions about what they read.

- The **Active Reading: Questions to Consider and Use** handout provides questions students can use before, during, and after reading. It identifies the reading skill required by each question.

- **Bookmark: Reading: Think A** provides reading reminders, a self-evaluation checklist, and space for writing questions, all on a handy bookmark. **Bookmark: Reading: Think B** helps less effective readers monitor their progress.

- The **Structured Response Notes** tool provides questions that help students organize and synthesize ideas about a passage, character, or text.

- The **Character Study** tool helps students ask questions and organize their ideas about character development.

- The **Literature Circle Notes: Overview of the Roles** and **Style Analysis Notes** handouts include questions for prompting discussion and analysis of literary texts.

- The **Four Core Questions** tool helps students focus on association, opposition, progression, and transformation of ideas. It can be used with many text types. The tool derives from Robert McMahon's **Summary of Basic Questions,** also in *Tools and Texts,* which is particularly helpful for evaluating characters in literature.

- The **Dense Question Strategy** handout helps students make different types of connections to a text to gather ideas for their own "dense question" about which to write an essay.

The **Text Tool** (above), the **Four Core Questions** tool (at the right), and the other listed tools are provided on the CD-ROM.

13 Use the Language of Literary Analysis

Students must know and be able to use appropriate literary terms when discussing or writing about literature.

Essential Skill Set

▶ **Read** the assigned text critically, focusing on the author's style.

▶ **Identify** and use appropriate analytical terms such as *tone*.

▶ **Apply** these terms when reading, writing, or talking about the text.

Frame the Lesson

THE SAT, ACT, ADVANCED PLACEMENT TESTS, AND ALL STATE TESTS expect students to know and be able to use appropriate literary terms when analyzing literature. It is often difficult for less experienced readers to generate the language needed to do this; others who know such terms struggle at the higher levels because the text is more nuanced, more complex. The freshman reading *To Kill a Mockingbird* can come up with the word *nostalgic* to describe the tone in the opening chapters far easier than most seniors reading the opening of *Crime and Punishment*. State and college entrance exams inevitably have questions such as "Which of the following words BEST describes the tone of this passage?" Students must be able to use literary language in the course of classroom discussions as fluently as when they write analytical essays or answer questions on a test. In this lesson my students learn to use "tone words" to describe Kate Chopin's tone in *The Awakening*.

Gather and Prepare

In the model lesson, I focus on tone, but The Language of Literary Analysis handout also covers style, mood, character, diction, and syntax words. Our text is the beginning of a brief novel, but you can use this lesson with any literary text. Choose a chapter or short text for introducing each technique so that students can locate examples efficiently. Introduce one technique at a time and repeat the sequence. Eventually, students will build up the vocabulary to talk about many techniques. The Language of Literary Analysis handout is a useful reference tool for kids to keep in their notebooks.

▶ Make copies of **The Language of Literary Analysis** handout for each student.

▶ After reading the model lesson, think about the text and the literary aspect you want your students to analyze. Make planning notes to adapt the lesson for your students and text.

▶ To use the **Reflective Reading Quiz** as noted in "Assess and Extend," modify it for the text and aspect your students are analyzing. Make copies for each student.

Within their group, Bijan and Eric evaluate the words they generated to describe an author's tone to find the best word, which one of them will then write on the overhead for the whole class to discuss.

Teach

WE'VE TALKED A LOT SO FAR ABOUT WHAT HAPPENS IN *The Awakening* and what it is about, but we need to read below these surface details to understand how Chopin creates this meaning and to find words we can use to describe what she does.

Today we are going to focus on using more specific language to discuss certain aspects of Chopin's *The Awakening*. The more precise our words, the more accurate our thoughts will be. Every discipline has a language you need to learn so that people understand what you are talking about when you are discussing a subject of mutual interest. Imagine two scientists standing around pointing at something on a slide. One says, "See that round thing there?" "What?" asks the other. "Do you mean the cell?" "Yeah, that thing," says the first. "Look at how it does *that*," he notes, to which his partner says, "What's 'that'? Are you talking about how it *divides*? That's called *cell division*." "Right, that's what I said," the other guy says. They wouldn't get far, would they? Using specific language makes communication much more effective. You will understand literature better as you learn and use the appropriate terms to talk about it.

You also need to know academic and literary terms for everything from the SAT and ACT to the state exams. You will often have a question like, "Which of the following terms BEST describes the main character in the story?" If you don't know the terms or how to apply such terms to the text you read, you will be lost. It's not about finding and using *bigger* words, but coming up with the *right* word.

First, we need to come up with some words, though! Last night you reread the opening of *The Awakening*, which deals mostly with the relationship between Edna Pontellier and her husband. You heard how the characters spoke to each other and about their situation, how the author spoke about them, how they acted, what they thought, felt, and so on. In your notebook, generate a list of ten words that describe the tone, or attitude, of the narrator toward Edna and of Edna toward herself. As you do this, try to think of examples in the text you could cite. For example, if you say she sounds "distant," you should be able to provide examples that show why you think *distant* is an apt term. You don't have to jot these details down, but you should have them in mind to defend your choice of words. Remember, if you get confused about what tone is, just think of the tone of voice your mother uses to call you when you are in trouble!

As the kids do this, I put a clean transparency on the overhead for them to write their final words on later. We use a transparency, or butcher paper if I am out of transparencies, so we can put the list of words up in the coming days as we discuss the novel. Writing the words on the board is too temporary. Plus sometimes I get distracted and leave the list up for the following period, and then the next class can just copy down the great words we generated the class before.

When you get ten words down, I want you to choose the *one* word that best describes the author's tone. Then take five minutes to gather some examples from the text to illustrate and support it. Make sure you include the page numbers so you can find your way back to those spots in the text. Then explain in a draft paragraph why this is the *best* word and how these examples support your claim. Just do this as a draft. No one has to feel any pressure about it, but it does need to be a paragraph because we're preparing for the next round of work.

Get kids thinking about using subject-specific language.

Help students generate words that describe the tone of the text.

Have students choose the best tone word and give them five minutes to explain their choice in a paragraph, followed by discussion.

I rarely have kids do any sort of unstructured freewrite, as they all seem to need intensive work at all levels on improving the organization of their writing.

Now that you have your paragraphs, I want you to get into groups and start sharing your words. Just do a quick whip-around in which everyone says their word—no need to read your paragraph or discuss why you think that is the best word. Actually, someone should jot these words down so you have them to refer to. Then, when you've finished going around, discuss each word and choose the *best* word from your group. Finally, prepare to explain why that word is the most appropriate to describe the tone of the opening.

As they are working, I pass out The Language of Literary Analysis handout. This is a list of words for concepts, such as tone, that we have periodically discussed but keep returning to since the concepts are abstract and elusive.

Find the list of "Tone Words" on The Language of Literary Analysis handout, and go through that list with your group. These are words that are commonly used to describe tone. Keep your word in mind, but go through this list and find three others that you had *not* thought about. When you have your three new words, evaluate them all and choose the *one* that is most precise.

When you come up with your word, send someone up to write it on the overhead. What if someone from another group writes the same word? That's fine. That will show the class that people agree about that word.

I allow a few minutes for students to come up and write their contributions on the overhead.

Now let's go through these words and use them to guide our discussion about the author's use of tone. Who put *ambivalent* up there? Let's start with that, since two groups thought that was a good description. Tell us why you chose it. Actually, why don't you start by describing what it *means*.

MAX: Well, we looked it up and it means that someone isn't sure how they feel about something.

That's a good start, Max, but it's worth clarifying it a bit. What is the prefix of the word *ambivalent*? It's *ambi-*. Does anyone know some words that begin with that prefix and what they mean? *(They come up with* ambiguous, ambitious, *and* ambidextrous.*)*

Those are good examples. What does it mean to be ambidextrous?

RACHEL: Doesn't it mean you can use either hand?

Yes. *Ambi-* means both sides. So if someone is ambidextrous, it means they can write with both hands. So, getting back to *ambivalent*—what does that mean?

RACHEL: I guess it means the speaker's tone suggests some sort of conflict, like they both like and don't like the character.

That's perfect. So look over the words we all collected on the overhead here, and choose the one you think best captures Chopin's tone. Then for homework, write a polished paragraph in which you analyze her tone, finding examples from the text to support and illustrate your claim. Bring that paragraph to class tomorrow, and we will pick it up from there.

The **Language of Literary Analysis** handout tool can be found on the CD-ROM.

Use The Language of Literary Analysis handout to expand the discussion and enhance their vocabulary.

Arthur and O'Brian add their words to the list on the overhead.

For homework, have students write a polished paragraph that analyzes Chopin's tone.

Assess and Extend

**If students need more support
with writing analytically…**

▶ **WRITE A COLLABORATIVE PARAGRAPH** If you are introducing this material for the first time or have students who need extra guidance, don't send them home to write. Instead, take the remaining time in class to write a structured paragraph together of academic prose using the word, details, quotations, and commentary. Have students complete this paragraph for homework if they still need more time.

**If students need test-readiness
practice…**

▶ **QUIZ STUDENTS ON TONE** Create a quiz on tone in general, and ask kids to apply that knowledge to this text in particular. (See the Reflective Reading Quiz template in *Tools and Texts*. Revise the template or create your own quiz to focus on tone in the text your students are reading.)

**If students are ready to
expand the lesson…**

▶ **LEARN MORE LITERARY TERMS** Repeat the sequence in this lesson to help students learn the language needed to analyze style, mood, character, diction, and syntax.

The **Reflective Reading Quiz** tool can be found on the CD-ROM.

*The drama of one's
own life and the
opportunity English
presents to explore that
drama through the
examination of one's
own and others' stories
foster a dramatic space.* "

—The English Teacher's Companion, p. 11

14 Analyze Character Development

Effective readers identify important character details and how they change as the story unfolds.

Essential Skill Set

▸ **Examine** how a character changes over the course of a story.

▸ **Identify** key character details established early in the story.

▸ **Evaluate** a character's behavior and emotions for important changes.

▸ **Analyze** causes, consequences, and significance of these changes.

Frame the Lesson

UNDERSTANDING CHARACTER IS CENTRAL TO UNDERSTANDING FICTION. *Character* is what drives a story. It is also what typically interests kids the most when they read stories. State and other standardized tests inevitably have questions about characters, many of which require students to make inferences about what kind of person a character is and who he or she eventually becomes. Most such tests include questions that ask, for example, "Which of the following words BEST describes the main character?" This lesson focuses on how to "read for character" while also preparing students to discuss and write about a character and how that character changes.

Gather and Prepare

In the model lesson, we're analyzing Edna Pontellier in Kate Chopin's *The Awakening* after students have read the novel. You can apply the same strategies and tools to any character in fiction, biography, or autobiography. The Character Arc can also be used during reading to track a character's evolution or as an organizer for writing, as described in "Assess and Extend."

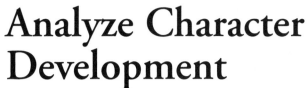

▸ Make copies of the **Character Arc** tool for each student.

▸ Have copies of **The Language of Literary Analysis** handout available for reference.

▸ Experiment with a Character Arc tool to plan your lesson and have as a resource. What should your students know about the character? When do critical changes occur? What passages should students discuss? What text references are helpful?

▸ Decide which "Assess and Extend" ideas fit your students. Prepare necessary tools and make copies for each student.

▸ Make planning notes to adapt the model lessson to your students and text.

Katie adds details to the Character Arc she creates through collaboration with her group as they examine how, when, and why the protagonist changes. She will use these notes to write an analytical paragraph.

Teach

Get kids thinking about character.

CHARACTER IS ONE OF THE MOST FASCINATING ASPECTS OF STORIES, but it's also an interesting idea. The word *character* itself comes from the Greek and means "to inscribe," or "the sharp end of a stick." It makes sense if you think about it: a letter in the alphabet is a "character" and has to be written with a pencil, that is, "a sharp stick." But it also raises an interesting question: If character is our personality, the essence of who we are, then is that "inscribed" into us? Is it written (with "the sharp end of a stick") into our DNA, our code? Or do *we* determine who we are? Do we write the code through our choices, which shape our personality? Or is it both? Character seems to be on people's minds a lot these days. A new book recently came out titled *Character Is Destiny*. The most looked-up word at *Merriam-Webster.com* this year was *integrity*—what do you make of that? Whether you think it comes from our DNA, our choices, or both, character is important.

Martin Luther King, Jr., said, "We should judge people by the content of their character, not the color of their skin." What do you think he meant?

I make room for discussion for a few minutes, posing questions to help students extend or clarify their thinking.

Write to make personal connections.

To think of it one other way, playwright Neil Simon said that when he is creating a character in a play, he merely keeps asking himself, "What does this character want more than anything else?" Simon says that, like characters in a play, we all reveal who we are—our character—through our desires, through the choices we make. Socrates had an interesting idea about this. He came up with the idea of the "ring of Gyges." Anyone ever heard of it? Quickly, he thought that you could tell what kind of person someone was by learning what he would do if he were invisible for twenty-four hours. Take a minute in your notebook to scribble down what you would do if you were invisible for twenty-four hours—and why you would do that.

When the students finish, we take a few minutes for an animated discussion and then follow up with a short extension of the assignment in which they draw conclusions about their character based on what they said they would do.

Use the Character Arc tool to analyze a fictional character.

All right, since you're *not* invisible, you have to get down to some work. So let's look at this idea of character. Here is a tool called the Character Arc. Many Hollywood writers use this as a tool to map out a character's changes over the course of a season. *(I ask Erik to pass them out for me while I draw a huge version on the board for us to build together.)* Here, on the far left, we need to establish what the character is like at the beginning of the story. Think of it as the beginning of the school year for you: What were you like? Or when you began high school—what words would you use to

The **Character Arc** tool can be found on the CD-ROM.

describe yourself then? We'll come back to that if we have time; for now, let's focus on Edna in *The Awakening*.

What are some adjectives we could use to describe Edna early on in the story? If you get stuck, turn to The Language of Literary Analysis handout and check the Character Words list. Call out your words, and I will jot them down on our arc here on the board.

As they call out adjectives, I list them. If a word is unclear, potentially wrong, or unique, I ask probing questions: "Why that word? How does that word relate to Edna? Can you provide some support from the text to back up your idea? Does anyone want to suggest a different word?"

Now, are some of these words more insightful or appropriate than others? Take a second and rank the top five—just put a number next to them (1–5) in order of relevance or accuracy.

Which one is the best? Take that word and make a statement about it. For example, I might choose *compliant* and write, "Edna begins the story as a compliant young wife and mother who fits the ideal for women of her time." Draft your statement about Edna first. Then go into the text and write the best five-minute paragraph you can, finding details and quotations in the text to support and illustrate your assertion about her character.

Okay, so what did you say? What word did you choose—and why?

After subsequent discussion…

Let's look at more of the text to see when, how, and why the main character changes. At what point would you say Edna changes? Actually, let me point out something I do when I am marking up my book, which you can do on sticky notes or in the margin if you mark it *lightly!* I make a little triangle symbol. Anyone know what that means? Think about scientific notations…. Right, it means *change*. So when I am reading and notice some major change—in the tone or a character, for example—I put in that symbol so I can come back to that part when I am writing or rereading. Now, let's get back to Edna. When would you say she starts to change?

After some discussion, we agree that the first shift in Edna's character occurs when she goes to the sea with Robert.

Okay, so let's make another division a little farther along the arc and generate another list of words to describe what Edna is like at that point. Let's use adjectives again so we are consistent with the first list. This will reinforce our recent discussions about parallel structure.

We list the new adjectives and then discuss the changes.

What *causes* these changes? What are the effects of these changes—on the character, the others, the plot? Are some changes more important than others?

After this discussion, depending on students' needs and our time, we may proceed to the next point of change. Several options are described in "Assess and Extend."

Brainstorm and write to describe the character at the beginning of the story.

Identify and describe the first point where the character changes.

BQs
. What is F.P. like?
. When does she change?
. Why does she change?
. How does she change?
. Which changes are most important?

Assess and Extend

If students need more help…

▶ **REINFORCE PERSONAL CONNECTIONS** If you have students who need more help understanding the abstract nature of character or simply don't immediately warm to the subject, have them first complete a Character Arc for themselves, beginning with some particular point in time and generating words to describe the kind of person they were then. Each point along the arc could represent a year in school, for example. Then have them use their arc as the basis for an essay in which they reflect on how they have changed over time and what caused those changes. Having completed this exploration, they could repeat the sequence for a character in the story you are reading.

If students have already
finished reading the book…

▶ **COMPLETE THE CHARACTER ARC TOOL** If students have finished the book, have them complete the sequence, moving along the Character Arc, indicating key changes in character by making a new line and generating a new list of words till they get to the far right and generate a list of words that sum up the character at the end of the story.

If students have not yet
finished the book…

▶ **ADD TO THE CHARACTER ARC** If students have not yet finished reading the story, have them add to their Character Arc as they read along, or you can periodically put the class arc up on the board and use it to facilitate discussion, having students add words and changes as they did today.

If students are ready to draft
a character essay…

▶ **APPLY TO WRITING** Once the Character Arc is completed, students have a rough outline for an essay that examines the character from the beginning to the end, each dividing line and list of words forming a potential paragraph. If students need additional structure and support to write this essay, consider using the **Character Development** tool.

If students need to analyze
character in more depth…

▶ **EXPAND ANALYSIS OF CHARACTER DEVELOPMENT** If you want kids to consider character in greater depth or from a different perspective, use the **Character Study** tool.

If students need test-readiness
practice…

▶ **USE A REFLECTIVE READING QUIZ** To combine character study and test-readiness, use the **Reflective Reading Quiz** template provided in *Tools and Texts*. Modify it for the character and text your students are studying. For an example, see the Reflective Reading Quiz Exemplar provided with the template.

The **Character Development** and **Character Study** tools can be found on the CD-ROM.

Analyze the Author's Style

Sophisticated readers examine how the author uses language and conventions to contribute to the meaning of the text.

Essential Skill Set

▶ **Identify** and explain how the author uses elements such as diction, imagery, conventions, syntax, or grammar to affect the meaning.

▶ **Analyze** the author's choices as they relate to his or her purpose.

▶ **Write** an effective literary analysis about the author's style.

Frame the Lesson

ANALYZING LITERATURE—ESPECIALLY SUCH ABSTRACT ASPECTS AS STYLE, TONE, OR THEME—is one of the more complex and thus difficult reading tasks students must perform. It is all the more difficult when they have to do it under the pressure of time on a state test or AP exam. They need a strategy they can apply reliably and efficiently to get inside the text and analyze what they find there so they can then write about or discuss it with precision and insight. This lesson focuses on examining an author's style, in particular the use of language and conventions and their contribution to a story's meaning.

Gather and Prepare

In the model lesson, my students analyze the author's style in Dostoevski's *Crime and Punishment*. The model notes on the Analytical Reading tool and the exemplars for two approaches to essay writing draw on this text. You can use the tool and exemplars with other literary texts by briefly explaining their source, or you can create your own versions based on the text your students are reading.

▶ After reading the model lesson, think about the text you will teach and decide what elements of the author's style your students should consider. Make notes on an Analytical Reading tool.

▶ Make copies of the **Analytical Reading** tool for each student. Also make an overhead transparency.

▶ Write exemplars and make copies or an overhead for students to read, or use the **Direct and Integrated Approaches Exemplars** provided in *Tools and Texts*.

▶ If you plan to expand the lesson, make copies of the **Style Analysis Notes** for each student. (See "Assess and Extend.")

The students discuss the assigned text, taking notes as they prepare to discuss and write about the author's style.

Teach

Get kids thinking about analyzing an author's style.

WE'VE BEEN TALKING A LOT ABOUT CHARACTER LATELY, but to fully understand and appreciate the craft of Dostoevski's story and how it all works together, we need to look at some other elements of the story such as the author's style and use of language. So I want to start spending a bit of time each day looking at a different aspect of the story and talking to you about how to write about that, also. Mostly, I want to talk about how to read analytically for now. Today we are going to look at style, which raises the obvious question of what to even consider when analyzing an author's style.

On the board, I write Style *and underline it to prepare for a list.*

Generate a list of elements that contribute to an author's style.

What sorts of things might you look at if you were examining an author's style?

The students call up a list of appropriate terms: grammar, diction, syntax, sentence length, and conventions. When Yvonne suggests commas, I pause and ask what she means and how she thinks commas distinguish an author's style. After she reads a few examples, I interrupt her politely to clarify that these are just the appropriate rules of comma use and thus do not constitute elements of style. She presses on, feeling that she has an idea she cannot get to. I suggest, "Why don't you bring that idea to your group, Yvonne—you will work in groups in just a second. Then try to explain to them what you are trying to say. They can help you figure that out, and you can present it to us later when we report back."

Show kids how to use the Analytical Reading tool to organize their analysis.

Before you get into your groups, I want to introduce a tool you can use to generate ideas for your analysis and organize it.

I pass out copies and put a transparency of the Analytical Reading tool on the overhead and shine it onto the whiteboard so it is large and I can write with a big marker in and around it.

Introduce the acronym MPE: meaning, purpose, effect.

When you analyze texts, you need a way to approach them strategically and in a way that will generate some organized response for writing. Here, you see in the Subject column a sample element of style based on *Crime and Punishment.* The acronym to get into your head—for when you *don't* have this handy tool available—is MPE: *meaning, purpose, effect.*

The **Analytical Reading** tool can be found on the CD-ROM.

So use this in your groups to help you think about the author's style in general and as it relates to your chosen character. *(Each group had to choose and become a specialist in one character, which they did previously.)*

They move into their groups and I let them settle into work, listening from my desk up front, a student desk like theirs that I turn to face them, to hear what they are saying. I also listen for those who might be struggling and assess the overall effectiveness of their work, making notes about how to follow up based on what they appear to need. I hear Kelley ask a question that might be of use to everyone, so I interrupt all the groups in my booming "teacher voice" to address my response to everyone. Then another student raises an important point.

SIBEL: Do we need to have quotations from the book?

You should always try to have examples from the book to support and illustrate what you mean.

CASEY: What do you mean "support and illustrate," Mr. Burke? Aren't those the same thing?

Good question. I use both because *support,* for me, means you need to prove some claim you are making, but *illustrate* means you need to show us what you mean. You might claim, for example, that Sonia is very meek, and so you would need to *show* what you mean. If, on the other hand, you argued that Sonia represents Martha in the biblical story of Lazarus, you would need to *support* that with some textual evidence. All right, now get back to work! You need to be ready to write in fifteen minutes.

Fifteen minutes later…

In a minute you will use what you discussed to help you write. We have been working on analytical writing. I wanted to just quickly show you two different ways to write about an author's style before you begin. These are just beginnings, samples to illustrate two approaches I want you to consider. The first one, the Direct Approach, lends itself more to the five-paragraph essay format, such as when a test like the AP exam asks you to "discuss diction, tone, and imagery." The Integrated Approach allows for a more sophisticated analysis because it looks at how the different elements interact with each other in relation to some point (about Raskolnikov in this case) you are trying to make. Use these sample paragraphs as you will to help you write your style analysis. Now, write!

Remind students that text references are necessary for analysis.

Share exemplars of two approaches to writing analytically.

The **Direct Approach and Integrated Approaches** can be found on the CD-ROM.

Assess and Extend

If students need more support for writing analytically...

▶ **DISCUSS THE EXEMPLARS** If style analysis is a new skill for the students, don't send them home to complete the writing assignment on their own, but instead walk them through the exemplars. I put my samples of direct and integrated paragraphs on the overhead projector to point to and discuss. Then I annotate and comment on what I did in each paragraph, how I did it, and why. In particular, I discuss my reservations about and limitations of the direct approach.

If students are ready to learn more about analyzing an author's style...

▶ **EXPAND THE LESSON** If students are beginning to show increased fluency in this kind of analytical reading, either introduce new aspects of style to examine in similar texts or have them analyze the same elements in a slightly more complicated text. Use the Style Analysis Notes handout to help students analyze the author's style in greater depth. If you have time, you can look at art or music to analyze style in ways they might find more concrete.

The **Style Analysis Notes** tool can be found on the CD-ROM.

> **Writing is the heart of the English class. It is here, in the drafts, notes, and clusters, that we watch our students compose their lives and try on different voices as they cast off one draft after another of themselves, in search of the voice they will recognize as their own."**
>
> *–The English Teacher's Companion,* p. 141

Tools can be found on the accompanying CD–ROM.

Texts marked with an asterisk (*) can be found in *Tools & Texts.* Other listed text titles are those used in Jim's model lessons and can typically be found in English classroom resource collections.

lessons 16–30

WRITING

Writing

LESSONS **16–30**

NOTES

continued on following page

Tools can be found on the accompanying CD–ROM.

Texts marked with an asterisk (*) can be found in *Tools & Texts*. Other listed text titles are those used in Jim's model lessons and can typically be found in English classroom resource collections.

Write to Describe

Effective writers use precise words and details to describe their subject.

> *Writing about personal importance is not to say students should always write about themselves; rather, they should write about subjects that challenge them to expand what matters to them, to connect who they are to what the world is becoming."*
>
> *—Writing Reminders, p. 35*

Essential Skill Set

▶ **Determine** your subject: a person, place, object, or event.

▶ **Generate** the appropriate language to describe your subject.

▶ **Evaluate** and choose the most compelling points about your subject.

▶ **Organize** the details in your description to support your main idea.

Frame the Lesson

DESCRIPTIVE WRITING SEEMS EASIER THAN OTHER FORMS because you can look at the subject and say what you see. Yet, when it comes to writing effective descriptions, many students have trouble knowing what to say, how to say it, and why they're saying it. Description relies on careful observation and analysis of those details that reveal something important about the subject.

Gather and Prepare

In the model lesson, my students and I write to describe two runners in a photograph from a news article, "Robo-Legs." While I was preparing to use the article for another lesson (Lesson 3: Develop a Purpose Question), I saw the photograph as a great opportunity to work on descriptive writing. Although the photo is not included with the article in *Tools and Texts,* you can find it online at scholastic.com, or you can easily adapt the lesson to help students write about other subjects. See "Assess and Extend" for more ideas.

▶ After reading the model lesson, choose a subject that you and your students will find interesting or helpful to describe.

▶ Make an overhead transparency of the photograph, image, or object if possible.

A group of boys huddles around a desk to generate language they can use to describe two runners in a photograph shown on the overhead projector. After filling their columns with words, they will use those words to write a detailed paragraph that describes the runners.

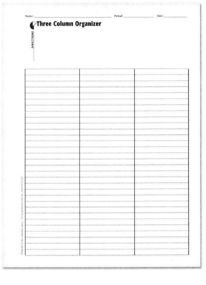

Teach

Get kids thinking about describing people in a photo.

I RECENTLY READ AN ARTICLE CALLED "ROBO-LEGS," WHICH DEALS with the incredible new technology involved in prosthetic limbs—that is, manufactured limbs. Here is the lead photo from the article.

I put the photo on the overhead briefly. It's a riveting photo of two boys with robotic legs running a race on a track.

Before we read the article, I want to use the photo as an opportunity to work on some descriptive writing and generate ideas and language while we're at it.

On an overhead transparency, I draw the following organizer. I could also use the Three-Column Organizer from Tools and Texts *for this purpose.*

Use a three-column chart to generate descriptive language.

First, take a sheet of paper and divide it into three columns, as I am doing on the overhead. Then keep adding to your chart as we fill in the chart on the overhead.

Okay, so what are some nouns we can use to describe what we see here? This is an incredible picture; these are remarkable boys! Let's just start with the obvious: What limbs are they missing?

ALEX: Arms and legs.

That's right. What are some nouns related to their robo-legs we can use?

"Metal."

"Technology."

"Running."

MONICA *chimes in:* No, *running* is not a noun.

Who thinks *running* is a noun? *(One student raises her hand. I press on, knowing exactly what they are all thinking.)*

How many of you think it's a verb? *(They all raise their hand.)*

Why is that?

Because it ends in –ing, *they explain, as if I'm the dumbest teacher they've ever had.*

Capitalize on opportunities to review and teach grammar points.

We can't take a lot of time on this, but let's quickly explain why the word *running* can be—all three types! If I ask Natalie, who is on the cross-country team, what her favorite sport is, her answer is a *noun* because it can function as the subject of my sentence. For example, "I love running," or "Running is the best sport." You can tell it's a noun because you can replace it with some other noun like "hot dogs."

What kind of shoes are you wearing there, Paul?

PAUL: Running shoes.

The **Three-Column Organizer** tool can be found on the CD-ROM.

Ah, so "running" is an *adjective* in that case because it is telling us what *kind* of shoes you are wearing—that is, it's an *adjective* modifying the *noun* shoes. Just like that pool outside the school: What kind of pool is that?

A swimming pool, *they say in chorus.*

So is *swimming* a noun, verb, or adjective in that case?

Adjective, *many say.*

Good! So here's the point I'm making: the part of speech is determined by how the word is used.

We go through a session of generating words for all three columns, working back and forth between the photograph and the organizer. When someone suggests a general word, such as happy *to describe a runner's face, we stop to generate other, more precise words, such as* joyful, ecstatic, *and* blissful. *If someone suggests a word that is not, for example, a verb, we stop to clarify and correct. Meanwhile, the writing is the main course here in this sequence, so we are pushing hard to get to that, using this brainstorming session to prepare to write.*

Now we have a wonderful set of words that you have generated and written down. I'll put the photograph back up here, and I want you to use those words to help you write a very detailed, descriptive paragraph about the runners. You don't have to use every word, but try to use as many as you can. Try to write in a way that captures the energy of the photograph, the emotion in the runners' faces.

We all settle down to write, myself included; I just sit in a desk as they do and use the same list of words. We write for ten minutes, interrupted periodically by questions and, on occasion, by the immature laughter of a few freshmen, who are a bit uncomfortable with the photograph because it shows a boy their age missing one arm and two legs. I make a point of not overwriting, so my example won't seem like showing off in this class of inexperienced writers. I'm just trying to join in on the community of writers and give the kids something to think about when we share our paragraphs.

Now trade your writing with a partner for a minute so you can see how others wrote about the same subject. *(After they do this, I read my paragraph aloud to share it with the class.)*

> *Pumping his one muscular arm, Cameron hurls himself toward the finish line, his eyes focused on his goal. His face radiates the joy of one who is doing what he thought he would never do again: running. Behind him another boy runs, his face wrinkled in concentration as he works to pass Cameron who has the lead as he reaches for the tape, his golden hair flying, his puka shell necklaces bouncing.*

All right, now we can actually read the article that will tell us about this boy and his incredible robo-legs! (See Lesson 3: Develop a Purpose Question.)

Write a paragraph that uses and organizes the descriptive details.

Share descriptive writing.

Students write for ten minutes using the descriptive words they generated.

Nouns	Adjectives	Verbs
metal		
technology		
running		

Assess and Extend

If students will benefit from
more practice with
descriptive writing…

▶ **EXTEND THE LESSON** To do more work on descriptive writing, have students go home and find an object that is important to them. "Importance" gives the writing a purpose, a focus that demands some persuasive thinking and makes it more interesting. Have students use another three-column organizer and then write a draft to work on in the coming days.

If students need to describe
complex subjects…

▶ **EXPAND THE LESSON** To help students describe a more abstract or complex idea (e.g., democracy, justice), take a more analytical approach. Identify the elements or ideas that are most important and then generate language to describe those elements in more visual, concrete terms than their abstract nature initially allows.

If students are ready to write
at higher levels…

▶ **ANALYZE AND WRITE DESCRIPTIVE ESSAYS** For a challenging and substantial unit on writing to describe, begin by reading a series of essays that describe different things and help students study them as models. For example, highlight specific words used to describe, and talk about how the author uses these words to capture the essence of the subject or make his or her point in the essay. Then let students choose a subject and write a descriptive essay using similar techniques.

Brianna, who lives for basketball, uses words she generated to describe the thrill of playing a basketball game before a crowd.

Write to Define

Defining is an essential skill for academic writing.

Essential Skill Set

▶ **Define** what words mean in the larger context of the essay.

▶ **Use** strategies like comparison and contrast to clarify and illustrate.

▶ **Provide** a range of examples of what the words do and do not mean.

▶ **Clarify** terms to improve specificity of definition.

Frame the Lesson

WE ARE ALWAYS STUDYING SUCCESS OF ONE FORM OR ANOTHER. "Who succeeds?" and "How?" are central questions to my classes. Within the context of school, the definition of success is often limited to academic success, yet academic success is merely a means to long-term success in the adult world for which we are preparing our students. This lesson asks students to draw on several readings and one activity to create a definition of success, which they then synthesize in a piece of writing. (For related lessons, see Lesson 6: Make Inferences About Deeper Meanings; Lesson 18: Write to Inform; Lesson 20: Begin an Essay; and Lesson 48: Study Traits of Successful People.)

Gather and Prepare

The topic of success is meaningful to all students. The model lesson focuses on financial success and uses a tool titled Traits That Contribute to Economic Success, provided in *Tools and Texts*. Ranking these factors leads to lively, relevant discussions. We follow up this activity by reading articles about other types of success. However, you can also use the lesson strategies to help students define any topic in your curriculum. Students can learn to use Target Notes whenever they are preparing to write a definition piece. A sample Target Notes tool is provided in *Tools and Texts*.

▶ After reading the model lesson, make a target tool to test the topic your students will define. Decide what texts, if any, will support your lesson.

▶ Make copies of Traits That Contribute to Economic Success or other texts your class will read. Prepare the materials to fit your lesson.

▶ Make copies of the **Target Notes** tool for each student if using the handout is preferable to drawing freehand.

Andrew and Michael work to define success by evaluating various factors that contribute to it. After ranking all the factors, they will post their top five choices on the board for subsequent class discussion.

Teach

Get kids thinking about defining "success."

Using Target Notes, identify and define types of success.

WE HAVE DISCUSSED SUCCESS THROUGHOUT MUCH OF THE YEAR, yet it is something one never fully understands, partly because there are different ways of achieving success. Today I want to use our time to do some classification thinking (that is, about *types* of success) and work toward a definition of what success is and how to achieve it.

On the board, I draw a Target Notes organizer and write "Types of Success" in the center. I tell the class to copy our notes out on binder paper to use later for the subsequent writing assignment.

What are the different *types* of success? We have talked often about one particular type, but it is certainly not the only type.

Academic success, says **JAMIL,** *seeming to tease me for I am a bit of a broken record about this. (I write "Academic" in one slice of the target.)*

Use strategies such as define by example and compare and contrast.

Definitely, academic success is something you need to keep your mind on as we move into the new semester. What other types of success come to mind? One way to think about this, if you are stuck, is to work backwards from some examples. Ask yourself, "Who do I think is really successful, and what type of success is that?" This is a way to define by example. You use an example to show by comparison and contrast how it is similar to or different from what you are trying to define.

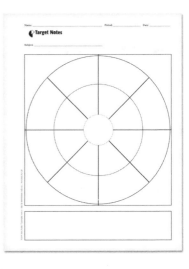

A sample **Target Notes** tool can be found on the CD-ROM.

Through a quick exchange of words and discussion, we arrive at the following types of success: academic, athletic, financial, political, personal, social, and business. No doubt, there are others, but this is a good list to work with, especially since my activity focuses on economic, or financial, success. We proceed to fill in the outer part of each section of the target to get an initial definition of each type—examples, details, and aspects of each type that we generate quickly and collaboratively. This is not the main course of our work today, so I don't take time for the kids to work in groups, though they might have a productive analytical discussion on the topic. This is all preparation for the thinking and writing they will do soon.

After identifying the most important factors, students post them on the board for subsequent class discussion.

Most of you would be willing to be millionaires, right?

They all call out some variation on, **Heck, yeah!**

I figured so. As it happens, I have read several articles lately about how people achieve financial success. So I put together a list of twenty-five factors commonly mentioned in these articles. I thought it would be interesting to look at that list a bit and then compare it to some other models of success. I cut the list up into strips and put the twenty-five factors in an envelope. You need to huddle up and rank them from 1 to 25 beginning with the one factor you think *most* leads to financial success. I want you to appoint someone to write the order down. I expect you to be able to explain why you ranked each factor as you did and *how it contributes to* someone's success.

Twenty minutes later, during which time I have been circulating, challenging, inquiring, guiding…

When you finish, have someone go to the board up front and list your group's top five factors. Be prepared to defend your choices and your ranking.

They all eventually head up to the board and list their choices numerically. Then we go through and discuss their choices and the rationales. This leads to a lively discussion.

Over the next few days, we follow up with a couple of short articles that offer different views of success in different domains. These articles are included in Tools and Texts. *"Walking Off the Fat, Across the Land" illustrates personal success. "Emmanuel Yeboah preps for Fitness Triathlon" illustrates athletic success along with social and personal success. "Find and Focus" addresses athletic and personal success. Then, to help students synthesize the definitions and types of success, I make a three-column organizer on the board. I could also give them the Three-Column Organizer included in* Tools and Texts.

What I want you to do now is use this chart to organize ideas for your definition of success. When you finish jotting down your notes, use them to write a one- to two-page paper whose purpose is to define what success is, incorporating and discussing different types, the various factors and how they contribute to success.

Have students rank and explain factors that contribute to financial success.

One student records the order in which her group ranked the factors of success. They will write their top five factors on the board. (See previous photo.)

Examine other types of success.

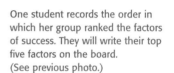

Types of Success	Examples (of what is and is **not** success)	Factors (that lead to success)
financial		

The **Three-Column Organizer** tool can be found on the CD-ROM.

Assess and Extend

If students are ready to incorporate related skills…

▶ **EXPAND THE LESSON** Use this occasion to revisit or introduce related skills, such as organizational patterns (least to most important) and comparative strategies such as point-counterpoint. You can also stress the value of defining what something *is* by showing what it is *not* and discussing why that person or example is not successful or does not embody an aspect of success.

If students need to work on basic writing skills…

▶ **REVISE THE WRITING** If students need to work on other aspects of writing, such as paragraph development or organization, have them use this piece of writing to do so, reworking it till they reach the standard that has been set as their goal.

If students are working on research skills…

▶ **GO INTO GREATER DEPTH** If this lesson is part of a unit on doing research and defining ideas (in greater depth), choose a person, team, company, or band and have students investigate that person's or organization's success, identifying the key elements and explaining what makes this person or company such a success.

If students need to practice public speaking…

▶ **SPEAK ON SUCCESS** Students can practice public speaking skills by offering up their own definition of success, drawing on their notes and reading to find details and examples to illustrate what they mean.

If students are ready to write independently…

▶ **DEFINE ANOTHER TERM** If students show adequate mastery of the skill of writing to define, let them choose their own word or concept and follow a similar process for writing to define that word or idea.

Kimberly, my aide, works with Louis and a small group to help them use their notes for the writing assignment.

> *"People must have something to say, something they care about, if they are to write well. Otherwise it is just an assignment. Thus another aspect of my approach is to always do my best to give kids some room to choose when it comes to what they write about."*
>
> *—Letters to a New Teacher, p. 41*

Write to Inform

Effective writers choose and organize details to inform readers about their topic in a way that changes or improves the readers' understanding of the subject.

Essential Skill Set

▶ **Decide** what topic you will inform your reader on.

▶ **Gather** important details on your topic that you can use to inform others.

▶ **Establish** a purpose when writing to inform.

▶ **Organize** and develop the details used to inform the reader.

Frame the Lesson

STUDENTS WRITE EXPOSITORY PROSE FOR ALL THEIR ACADEMIC CLASSES and on all state and national exams. Pressure to write well has increasingly severe consequences if they cannot do it. While some topics (e.g., describe a place or a person) are generic, many academic prompts or assignments demand that students gather and use information from one or more texts to write their essay. This lesson—part of a larger unit that culminates in a paper or speech about a person, experience, or event that students have researched—focuses on drawing conclusions from and finding supporting details in an article about Abraham Lincoln.

Gather and Prepare

In the model lesson, my students read "Leaders and Success: Abraham Lincoln" as they prepare to write an informative paragraph about qualities that made Lincoln successful. This article is provided in *Tools and Texts*, or you can use the "collaborative reading" strategy in this lesson with any informational text and writing assignment that fit your kids and curriculum. A brief article or passage that can be read in one class period works best for introducing the strategy.

▶ After reading the model lesson, consider the text your students will read and annotate. Note points you want to be sure they notice.

▶ Make copies of the article or text for each student. Make an overhead transparency of the first page (or more) to use as a model for collaborative reading.

Krish and Louis engage in collaborative reading of an article about Abraham Lincoln, during which they annotate each paragraph. They will use their annotations as the basis for a piece of informational writing about Lincoln.

Teach

Help kids make connections to writing to inform.

WE ARE MOVING TOWARD A PAPER, WHICH YOU WILL ALSO USE as the basis for a speech eventually, that requires you to investigate someone worth studying. This "Life Study" unit is an idea I came up with from reading a newspaper recently. The editors have an ongoing column called "Leaders and Success," and every day they feature a different person. Recently they ran a column about Lincoln, which was great because I've been listening to a fantastic book about Lincoln on my iPod on the way to work every day lately.

Jamil is passing out the article. While he does that, you can get out some paper and a pencil, and a highlighter if you wish but it's not necessary. *(While they do this, I put a transparency of the first page of the article up on the overhead.)*

Identify the topic kids will focus on.

Today I want to just focus on how to gather information to use when writing to inform. You are going to read to identify the qualities Lincoln had—according to the article—that made him a success. For the record, every year Lincoln is routinely voted the most respected of all our presidents.

Model collaborative reading.

I want you to use a technique I call collaborative reading. What you do is pair up and read each paragraph to identify the quality that is the focus of that paragraph, and then identify an example of that quality in action. If, for example, you read a paragraph and think that its main point is that Lincoln was ambitious, you would write *ambitious* in the margin and then underline an example or some other detail related to his ambition in the paragraph. Let's look at the article on the overhead, and I'll show you what I mean.

I read the first paragraph, a single lead line.

I'm going to ignore that line because it doesn't have anything in it related to the question we are trying to answer. Someone read that second paragraph there.

NICK *reads:* "And then there was Abraham Lincoln. Complaining didn't occur to him—not when he could take the same disadvantages and make them opportunities."

Thank you, Mr. Cohn. Well read. Is there something in this paragraph that contributed to his success?

NICK: Oh, yes, he was, um…what do you call that? Like when you have a positive outlook on things?

Optimistic?

NICK: Yes! That's it. He was optimistic.

Excellent—and a good word to use. So now underline the sentence or phrase in the paragraph that is an example of his optimism. *(I wait while they do this.)*

What did you underline?

ALEXANDRA: "Take the same disadvantages and make them opportunities."

There you go! Let's do one more to make sure we all have this strategy down. Remember, our PQ—purpose question—is, "What traits led to Lincoln's success as a leader?"

After working through one more paragraph, they show they understand the technique and the task, so I can let them move ahead.

Go ahead and read the rest of the article, stopping after *each* paragraph to determine one word that sums up what the writers are saying about Lincoln's success. Then write that word in the margin. If you get stuck, ask for help. If you can't think of the word, call me over and we can work on it together. Then underline the examples in the paragraph. That's very important, as you will need those underlined details when you finish.

For the next stretch of time, they work collaboratively and I circulate, stopping to monitor how they work and what words they put down. If someone writes a vague term in the margin, I ask what other words they could use to be more precise.

Okay, now everyone's pretty much finished. You have a list of qualities about successful people and Lincoln in particular, along with details in the paragraphs that you can draw on. Before we move ahead, go through and choose—highlight or circle them, it doesn't matter—the three qualities that are most important from the words in the margin.

Now I want you to use the three details you highlighted in the margin of the Lincoln article as the basis for your own paragraph. Arrange those in the order of importance. Then work those details you underlined into your paragraph as examples of what you're saying.

I let them write until a few minutes before the end of class.

That's good work for a day of class. You read an article about Lincoln and did some good writing. We'll come back to your ideas tomorrow. We're just getting started on this unit, but keep in mind the things you read today. These are not only reasons why *Lincoln* was successful but why successful people in general succeed. Start thinking about someone you want to study and write about in your upcoming paper.

Louis uses the notes he generated with Krish to write his paragraph about Lincoln.

Have students read collaboratively to gather more details.

Write about three qualities of success.

LEADERS AND SUCCESS: Abraham Lincoln: His Aim? Liberty And Justice
By Michael Mink (*Investor's Business Daily*, February 13, 2005)
Source: http://www.investors.com/editorial/lands.asp?view=1
Directions
1. In pairs, read each paragraph.
2. *After reading a paragraph,* write an adjective that best describes Lincoln as he is described in that paragraph.
3. *Before moving on to the next paragraph,* underline words in the paragraph that relate to that adjective.
4. When you finish the article, circle the five most important adjectives.
5. Use the sample and guidelines from page 68 of the *Reader's Handbook* to write a paragraph. Be sure your paragraph has a **focus, organization,** and **development** Use the List Order format. Be sure your paragraph relate to the main idea (**focus**) of your paragraph). (examples and discussion of how examples relate to the main idea (**focus**) of your paragraph).

When faced with disadvantages, some people complain.

And then there was Abraham Lincoln. Complaining didn't occur to him — not when he could take the same disadvantages and make them opportunities.

The biggest obstacle Lincoln (1809-65) had to overcome was his own humble beginnings. Born into poverty, to illiterate parents, his formal schooling totaled less than a year. But he had a powerful ambition to achieve, and a yearning to make the world a better place.

The answer for Lincoln was literally all there in black and white, in the form of the books he learned to cherish. As a boy, he resolved to educate himself. As a man, he never stopped adding to his store of knowledge.

"The mode is very simple...
study them carefully...
for reading...

Assess and Extend

If students are beginning a research project...

▶ **EXPAND THE LESSON** If students need to begin researching a topic, do a workshop on how to do research on the computer. Also see Lesson 27: Synthesize Multiple Sources.

If students are ready to write more than one paragraph...

▶ **TEACH STRATEGIES FOR ORGANIZING INFORMATION** If students have completed their research and have the information they need to write, use a tool like the **Main Idea Organizer** or an outline to help them shape it into a form from which they can write a draft. To teach or review organizational strategies, see the **Organizational Patterns** and **Academic Writing** handouts in *Tools and Texts*.

If students need further practice with gathering details...

▶ **REPEAT THE SEQUENCE WITH OTHER ARTICLES** If students show some need to further study how to extract and organize information before writing to inform others about their subject, use similar articles and follow this lesson sequence until students can apply the skills independently.

If students need more support with drawing conclusions...

▶ **REVIEW HOW TO DRAW CONCLUSIONS** If students have trouble drawing conclusions to determine the qualities that contributed to Lincoln's success, refer to Lesson 5: Draw Conclusions from What You Read.

The **Organizational Patterns** and **Academic Writing** tools can be found on the CD-ROM.

Dan writes about Tom Landry, legendary football coach, to show his mastery of the sequence and as part of our Life Studies Unit.

19

Develop a Topic

Writers generate a range of possible topics and choose the one that has the best potential.

The Target Notes *tool begins by asking the student to consider what is at the center of the inquiry. What is the student 'aiming' at? The two strands of the target invite scaffolding of thought: the first strand calls for identifying categories or perspectives, which are then developed through examples, details, or quotations in the outer strand."*

—Tools for Thought, p. 97

Essential Skill Set

▶ **Understand** the writing prompt.

▶ **Generate** a list of possible topics.

▶ **Choose** the most appropriate topic.

▶ **Generate** and organize details to use when writing about this topic.

 The **Target Notes** tool can be found on the CD-ROM.

Frame the Lesson

KIDS OFTEN SIT DOWN TO WRITE ABOUT A TOPIC THEY DID NOT CHOOSE and that they struggle to understand, perhaps because it has no connection to their own lives. We can address this in our classes by giving students choices whenever possible. On state tests, however, they have little or no choice and must be able to generate topics in response to prompts that are often abstract or not interesting. This sequence shows you one way to help kids develop a topic; the technique can be adapted for use with other topics.

Gather and Prepare

In the model lesson, my students write about someone who has influenced their lives. I model for them how to use the Target Notes tool to identify several possible topics (people who have influenced them), choose one topic, and develop that topic with ideas they will use to write about one significant person. This is a meaningful assignment and a good way to introduce the tool. However, you can use the Target Notes tool to help students develop a topic from any prompt or assignment. Adapt the tool to fit the topic and your students' abilities. For example, I divide the target into six sections for this lesson. See the following lessons for other ways to use Target Notes: Lesson 17: Write to Define; Lesson 21: Craft an Effective Argument; and Lesson 42: Identify and Prepare a Speech.

▶ After reading the model lesson, consider the prompt or assignment you will give your students and use the Target Notes tool to explore the topic. Adapt the tool as needed and fill out a copy to draw from when you model the process.

▶ Make copies of the **Target Notes** tool for each student. Make an overhead transparency of the tool to fill in during the lesson.

Nick generates different possible topics, working through each category on the Target Notes tool before entering into discussion with others. Eventually, he will choose one topic and develop that into his essay.

Help kids connect to generating ideas.

Explain the prompt and the Target Notes tool.

Model how to generate topics to write in the target.

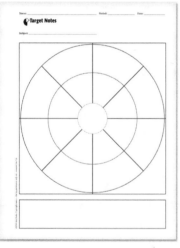

The **Target Notes** tool can be found on the CD-ROM.

Model how to write details and examples in the outer strand.

Model how to choose the best topic.

Teach

MARK TWAIN SAID WRITING IS LIKE SENDING A BUCKET DOWN into the well to bring up ideas—sometimes the bucket comes up empty. When that happens, he knows that it's time to get out and read, talk to people, or (his favorite) take a steamboat trip on the Mississippi River to refill the well with new material for stories. Everyone has a tough time getting started, especially when you are taking a big test and you don't know what the prompt will be. That's the worst! But today we are going to talk about something you can do to make sure you come up with a good topic and a quick working idea of what to say about it.

Let's say you have this prompt you have to write about: "Choose a person who has had a major influence on you and explain how they have influenced you." It's a topic you might have to write about for a class, on a writing test, or on a college application. It's also something worth thinking about. Let's call it our Roundtable of Influence, and we will use this Target Notes tool to help us come up with ideas.

Write your own name in the middle of the target. Though you're still young, you have a lot of people who have influenced you in different ways. They don't have to be people you even like. For example, I could tell you that one of the worst teachers I ever had taught me more than most about what a good teacher should do. They don't have to be people you know, either. Authors and people I've read about all influence me in various ways. Instead of immediately writing names in the eight slots, the inner strand, on the target, make a list of many possible names in the margin.

Ask yourself which SIX of those people have had the biggest influence on you. Some of them might not be people in your life now. I could say that my tennis coach when I was twelve had a profound influence on me—even to this day, though I have not seen him in thirty years. I could also say it was the author of a book I am listening to on my iPod in the car on the way to work right now.

Once you have filled in those six names in the inner slots, jot down a quick explanation of *how* each person has influenced you. It can be a few words or a sentence. I might say, for example, that Mike Rose taught me, through his books, that "everyone can learn to be successful in school if someone shows them how." Or in the box linked to my father, I might write words like "integrity, humility, hard work, values" to indicate some of the values my father taught me.

So, in the outer part of the target, I'm going to jot down examples and details of these different influences. I might also jot down why each person's influence was so important; in other words, I might explain why they are one of the six people at my Roundtable of Influence. *(My model is shown in "Assess and Extend.")*

Finally, I choose the one person who interests me the most and about whom I can write the best essay. Let's say, for example, that I choose my father. I might choose him not only because he is such an important influence—still, even though he died more than a decade ago—but also because I have such good stories to use in the essay. I can talk about how we worked into the night in the workshop and the lessons he taught me about making things, the importance of doing things the right way. Or I